HE **RESTORES** MY **SOUL**

THE JOURNEY OF A SERVANT

RANDY S. DEAN, SR.

FORWARD By
Bishop Parnell M. Lovelace, Jr.

CONTENTS

Forward

He Restores My Soul is a guide and support to those of us who have the heart of serving others. Randy Steven Dean, Sr. takes a candid and difficult look into the dark side of ministry. He moves quickly past the external stimulus that often attracts people to the ministry and addresses the underlying factors that malign and misguide our life choices. It has been said that one of the most vulnerable and difficult professions is that of serving within the clergy. The woman and man, daring to heed the call of God, must be willing to explore a remarkable introspective evaluation of one's personal, pastoral, professional, and potential life. Such observations reveal our brokenness, our damage, our frustrations, and our sinful propensities. Yet, it is also within this state and posture that

God the Father exudes immeasurable grace and demonstrates His unconditional love. Randy captures this process through sharing his own explorative journey. He, with great transparency, invites all that would be healed and renewed, to open their hearts to a loving perfect God, who has chosen to use the imperfect as vessels of compassion. Be warned: All who read this writing will be encouraged to *step back* and *grow* forward. Indeed there is a light at the end of the tunnel. One may find that it is not a train approaching head on, but rather the love of God that indeed restores our soul.

Parnell M. Lovelace, Jr., MSW MPTH
Senior Pastor of Center of Praise Ministries, Sacramento, California

ACKNOWLEDGEMENTS

I would like to first, thank and give all of my gratitude and praise to God for allowing me to express my story, that I hope honors Him in the most prolific form. I am grateful for His patience with me and my many shortcomings over the span of my lifetime. I thank Him for not giving up on me even when I gave up on Him and myself. I dedicate this book to the strongest woman I have ever known, my mother (Arline Dean). She has battled the disease of multiple sclerosis for over two decades and yet she has been the epitome of faith and positive thinking. She has overcome so many negative things in her lifetime and still draws from her well to inspire her family, friends and anyone she meets, to persevere. Thank you mom, I love you with everything in me.

I dedicate this book to the two gifts God gave me, my children Steven and Ashli. Your commitment to love me beyond all that has happened has encouraged me in ways that defy expectation. You are the reason I smile today. Thank you for encouraging me to push this project to completion. I can't wait to see what God will continue to do through you both.

I also dedicate this book to my family, who has watched me transition in and out of so many situations over the years and yet loved me and supported me even if they never fully understood what I was doing. I want to thank and acknowledge my Grandmother (Missionary Augusta Finch) who took me in when I was literally homeless, trying to start my life over again. I found out spending time with her, where the gift of writing began, she has written and it transcended to my mother and now I can say I truly got it honestly. Lastly, thank you to all of my friends who have remained my friends despite the times of silence or distance and even disagreements. Thank you all so much, I love you deeply.

HE RESTORES MY SOUL

INTRODUCTION

The Lord is my shepherd I shall not want. He makes me to lie down in green pastures. He leads me beside still waters. He restores my soul. He leads me in the paths of righteousness for His name's sake. Even though I walk through the valley of the shadow of death I will fear no evil. For you are with me, Your rod and Your staff, they comfort me. You prepare a table before me in the presence of my enemies. You anoint my head with oil; my cup runs over. Surely goodness and mercy shall follow me all the days of my life and I will dwell in the house of the Lord forever...

Psalm 23 is probably one of the most beloved and quoted scriptures in the Bible. Its message offers great comfort and assurance to the reader. We memorize its verses because they speak to our challenges as well as our emotional and spiritual states of mind. Its language is simplistic in form so that children in Sunday school and Christian circles arouse our approval with their memorization of the famous writing. While it's much easier to find comfort and faith through the words coined so many years ago, I often wonder, do we really understand its significance and are we able to fully embrace the depth of the message that lies beneath the written text.

In David's assertion "He restores my soul" there are two primary suggestions that we can glean and conclude that will be addressed in this book:

1. The term "restores" which used in its proper context suggests not the ending of a restoration process, but rather the continuation of it.

2. To restore something suggests a previous state of unacceptable existence such as a car that was once the premier example of innovation and is now merely a rusted shadow of its potential.

What state is God's desire to restoring our life?

The purpose of this book is to bring a sense of awareness to not only the inherent challenges of the church, but also to those who seek to walk closely with God bringing you to an understanding of His intent to see your life fully healed and restored from any emotional or spiritual damage, you may have sustained through the experience we call life. It is also deliberate in encouraging and strengthening your faith in your journey and promoting complete transparency with God and accountability with other like-minded believers. This book is not designed to be the end all to every situation that has brought devastation and challenge to your life, but rather to offer an array of hope and encouragement to whatever you may have faced, are facing, or will face. Much of what you will read is based on many personal experiences and the lessons learned coming through them. What good are life's challenges unless wisdom is gained from them. It is my attempt to dispel many of the myths that have afflicted our churches and more specifically the expectations we place upon them. From the pulpit to the pew, we will examine the many issues that have served to cripple our effectiveness as believers in God and the Lord Jesus Christ and in many cases, damaged or destroyed our witnessing.

When you think of a victim, what picture comes to your mind? Most, if not all people see the person that was the object of hurt as a victim. That of course is for example the obvious answer; however, it is not the full picture. It is very easy to conclude that the rape victim, the physically abused, and the sexually molested as victims. We see the unfaithful spouse, the drug addict, the alcoholic, and the thief as perpetrators, not victims. Not removing responsibility from those who have committed such devastating actions, we will look deeper into the product of a fallen man and examine how God in His sovereignty will and can restore anyone. The reality of human existence is that we have all sinned and fallen short of the glory of God (Romans 3:23). With that being said, the difference between one who has perpetrated hurtful acts and those who have suffered the hurt in many cases are those who have addressed the deeper issues that surround their lives.

If you have ever questioned the validity of the Christian faith and the church experience, please continue to read. If you have ever wondered if what you have lived through in church has left you feeling empty, hopeless, or challenged, I encourage you to allow the words of this book to penetrate your thoughts and consider the wisdom of God and His ability to reach beyond the prevailing thoughts of our fears and inadequacies. Do you ever feel or have you ever felt that you are not qualified to be even called a child of God because of mistakes you have made or the damage you may have caused in the lives of others? What about feelings of inadequacy due to the harm that has happened to you?

CHAPTER ONE

CONFLICT IN THE KINGDOM

I once attended a Pastors' conference in Florida that was geared towards supporting the
needs of men and women who carried the
responsibility of such an esteemed position in
the church. I heard the host of the conference, Bishop T.D. Jakes, make a statement that
referred to a message he recently taught. As I
sat in a large room of over three hundred Pastors and spouse, feeling a bit relieved by the
support of my constituents and at the same
time I felt like an outsider and an outcast. I
was in the room with men that bore the same
mantel of responsibility that I carried and yet I
couldn't seem to shake the feeling that I was
somehow an isolated case unqualified to call

myself a Pastor. It often amazes me how you can be in a room filled with people and yet feel alone. Conferences can often heighten that feeling, though it is meant to promote unity and support. The comment Bishop made was met with a resounding sense of awe or perhaps it was simply in my mind as I heard him say, "There's a king in every kid and a kid in every king". "Boy is that profound," I thought as I searched deeply for meaning and understanding in his words. Have you ever heard something so enticing that you grasped at it without fully understanding its meaning?

I pondered over that statement for the entire three days of the conference as I observed my fellow brothers and sisters in many unspoken dilemmas and challenges that seemed to fill the atmosphere. No one seemed to say a word concerning the personal issues that we were all obviously there to somehow address back home. Yet there was a sense of outcry in the room where we sat. Hunger for words to bring a sense of ease, fulfillment and righteousness were the unspoken expectations. Indeed there was an elephant in the room. At one point during the conference, they separated the men and women into two groups. The purpose was clear, which was to offer a safe environment that encouraged transparency of personal challenge and promote healing within the groups. Even after the gallant effort to produce such a healthy outcome, there was little to no takers. No one seemed to want to expose his or her wounds and/or weaknesses. It appeared that everyone walked away the same way they came. We met new friends, established great networking, and enjoyed one another's company. But what internal work was really accomplished? Like many, I am sure I wanted so deeply to hear or experience something that would make it all go away. After all, isn't that why we attend such inspirational events? Don't we seek such events to somehow help us to transition the disparity in our lives into a relevant tool of our past? I think most of us, at some point in our lives, whether attending our church services or living our daily lives often send up the same sentiment towards heaven, "Lord, just make it go away!".

I continued in deep thought over the Bishop's statement and what began to emerge was what I call the transitions of life. The king in the kid, to me, spoke to three areas from the child's perspective: **potential, purpose, and power**. To begin with, potential is a picture of what lies within but has yet to be brought out. It starts with a thought or sensing of something great that is destined for success such as an idea, a career, a business, an endeavor or even a relationship and needs to be discovered and nurtured within the child and brought forth. Potential is something that you are born with. It is not taught but rather illuminated and extracted. It cannot be purchased or prayed for, you were born with it. The discovery of potential brings us to a place of awareness or more accurately, purpose. Purpose gives us reason for existence and becomes the drive to move us forward in helping us succeed in life. When purpose flees our life, hopelessness often sets in. Everyone needs to feel or understand their purpose. You can spend so much of your life trying to discover your purpose and in the process you feel completely lost. Often when someone does not understand their purpose they look to find it in others. Once potential and purpose are revealed we can then move into the final area of this thought which is power or authority. Power becomes the tool that builds our confidence to fulfill our soaring potential. Without power, there can be no success in reaching the pinnacles of our goals and objectives. Everything responds to power because power trumps obstacle. But if you don't understand that you have power to achieve your goals and ambitions, you will not overcome the obstacles that may confront your life. The Apostle Paul summed up that thought with an emphatic statement, *"I can do all things through Christ who strengthens me"* (Phil. 4:19).

These three areas are what gives every king or queen their significance in the kingdom they command. The kingdom they govern consumes their life. What everyone benefits from is the years of grooming, education, and nurturing of the future Heirs to the throne. They don't grow up wondering what their potential, purpose, and power are here on earth. They are made aware of it from childhood and reminded through adulthood. Both distant and recent history has taught us that no kingdom is without conflict.

The Apostle Paul stated, *"When I was a child I spoke as a child, I understood as a child, I thought as a child; but when I became a man I put away childish things"* (I Corinthians 13:11 NKJV).

Evolving is what the message suggests and articulates. But what happens when there is no one to help a child discover his or her purpose or no one is there to nurture his or her potential? What happens when the child has been the object of emotional, sexual, or physical abuse? If the child is left to deal with the ungodly, inhumane or neglectful experiences and their affects alone, what kind of king or queen will they turn out to be? What kind of husband or wife will they become? What kind of parent will they be? What kind of friend will they be? What kind of Pastor or church worker will they be? Most importantly, what kind of child of God will he or she develop into?

You may look at this and say, "I am no King or Queen". Most of us are not, however, we are all children of a King (our creator) and we all have a circle of people who are influenced and affected by the outcome of our lives and the choices we make, both the good and the bad, whether it is merely 10 people or 10 million people. Your life matters. Let me say that again... Your life matters.

We can often deflate into the backdrop of life when we lose that very perspective. Who we become is reflective of where we've been. At the very least there is always an influence on our character and ways that are mirrored from our past. Everything is affected, how we think and act and interact with people and challenges, even how we interact with God is affected. Our tendencies toward God are often tainted by the impact that people have had in our lives. People you once felt close to in your life that may have hurt, abandoned, or betrayed you can become a part of that challenge in your relationship with God. This conflict seemingly becomes more evident as you learn to trust in a God who is not seen through natural eyes yet encourages you to draw closer to Him. This is clearly why God has continually expressed Himself in the Bible as not being the same as man. As He has stated, "He is not a man that He should lie" (Numbers 23:19 NKJV). God certainly wants to be distinguished as the creator of man and is able to relate to man, but is not the same as man. We were created in His image and likeness; He was not created in ours.

Jesus once stated that *"the kingdom of heaven suffers violence and the violent take it by force"* (Matthew 11:12 NKJV).

Success in any kingdom whether heavenly or earthly, is not absent of conflict. If you examine the Bible closely it is filled with stories of not merely successes but conflicts that bring about success. Life is filled with conflict and it is in the place of conflict that helps us learn about who we really are. If you really want to find out how much character you possess allow conflict to arise in your life. But one of the greatest challenges we face is when we are in a place we don't expect conflict to exist. The church is the last place you look to find any level of conflict. This misplaced perception has often caused many to drift not only from the church, but also from their faith in God. Even the healthiest church will have some level of conflict within it.

Let's take a look at families for example. The statement I often hear when speaking with people concerning their personality challenges is usually along the lines of "I come from a dysfunctional family". My response to that statement is always "tell me whose family isn't dysfunctional?" Everyone has some degree of dysfunction in his or her family. If you doubt my words, wait until you attend your next family reunion... The more accurate assessment would be to state that we come from either a healthy family or an unhealthy family. The difference between the healthy family and the unhealthy family is how that family handles the crisis or problems that they face. That being said, if we collectively come from families that face conflicts and problems through everyday life, what makes us think that when we put all of those wonderful people together in a building we call a church, we won't have any issues?

Families make up the sum total of our churches. Without families there would be no churches and without churches, communities suffer the greatest. Likewise, strong churches make up strong communities.

There is no such thing as a "perfect" church because there is no such thing as the perfect person. The church is either healthy or unhealthy. To put it quite simply, the church is a product of its members. So please don't waste years, jumping from one church to another in search of perfection. Trust me, you won't find it. Look for a healthy church that will speak healthy things into your life, that address your mind, body, and spirit and guide you in the truth of God's word. Life is filled with conflict and, as much as we may not want to deal with some of its greatest challenges, conflict can be healthy. Conflict is necessary to right things that are often wrong in life. Sometimes the most challenging conflict has nothing to do with the people we work with or who are in our families, schools, jobs or churches. Sometimes the greatest conflict we can face arises within ourselves. Those are often the battles within that we may be reluctant to address. It can often feel like a buried land mine that lies deep within. We know it's there somewhere, but we are afraid to take the wrong step in fear that we may move in that one spot and face sudden detonation. In our state of mind, we are either healthy or unhealthy.

The recent wars in Iraq and Afghanistan pales in comparison to what conflicts we often face within ourselves. The end of the war for many veterans seemed to never have concluded once their tour ended in a war zone. For many of them, it continues for years passed their time serving their country. The internal war and a desire for resolve and peace continues to weigh heavily in their minds. They grapple with things that they saw in battle that were neither natural nor expected.

In the pursuit of becoming what we may believe we were created to be, we are often faced with a mirrored image of someone we feel falls short of that final picture. Many of us frequently look for outside sources to validate what God has placed within us to become. Since we sometimes struggle to find fulfillment within how God sees us, we look for our contentment of what we "should" look like in others. One of the greatest challenges can often be seen when we look at the kings and queens in entertainment circles, church circles, community circles, sport arenas and public servant circles. We admire their lifestyles and successes and mentally gauge ourselves based on what we see in them. It's one thing to admire someone else's success and be inspired by what they do or have become, it's another thing to envy it. When admiration turns to envy, bitterness is always around the corner. When one lacks internal peace and contentment, envy becomes the temptation that darkens the doorpost of their heart. Peace and conflict cannot coexist. We are either in a state of peace or a state of conflict.

If one of my children needs to find out what I expect of them or see in them, they come to me to find out. If they rely on each other or other avenues to get the information they need to inspire them then something will lack because it did not come from the source of where they needed it most; their parent. There are some things that only a parent can give their children. The same is true of God. If we really want to find peace within ourselves then we must go to God to get the peace we need. If you want to find out your purpose in life, you must go to the One who gave you your purpose before you were born. This is where we often come up short. We often seek to find meaning in the expression of others and circumstances instead of the one who is the creator of purpose, God. If we really believe that He exists, and is all knowing, then we must be willing to seek Him and trust Him for greater understanding of what He has purposed and planned for our lives.

Processing the Kingdom

This brings me to the next point which is simply process. One of the things I have often shared is concerning God's process. Since our western culture and American society are driven by instant results, instant change, instant food, instant money, instant weight loss, instant love and instant outcomes, it is understandable why we expect the same things from God. Our greatest disappointment comes when what we say we believe God for does not happen in the time or manner we expect. God does not operate like your microwave. He is not going to just materialize the results we are expecting in the way we expect it because that's what we want. God is not a formula you can just work out or think that saying a few magical phrases or demonstrative gestures is going to change how He moves in your life or situations. We must give place to His sovereignty and trust His will and ways for our lives if we are to see His best worked out for us.

The process is designed to address two things: how you think and how you speak. Our mind is where it all begins. We literally rise or fall based on our mindset and our perception. It is the only difference between people who have succeeded in life and those who have left this earth never having tapped into their potential.

The first thing we must understand about process is that not only is it applicable to our lives, it is in theory a principle of life. Everything is a process, which simply means it is a coop-erative effort. It is God's desire working with our willingness. Beginning with how the earth was created by God and including everything He placed in our world, nothing just "appears", everything has a process for coming into existence. Don't get caught up merely in the outcome of things, seek to understand its process and you will appreciate the outcome even more. Inner conflict is often a result of our learning to surrender our will to God and embracing His will. Process is where what is right is confronted by things that are wrong within us. Two opposing thoughts or ideas equal conflict. It is the place that illuminates the measure of integrity we really possess versus what others see in us. Your character is chiseled through conflict, yet what is most desirable is the outcome not the process. This is because process is sometimes painful. What we admire most of people is the perceived outcome of where they have succeeded in their lives. It is much easier to hear of an individual's struggles and conflicts rather than to have lived it ourselves.

When I was younger there were things that I did not value like I do today. Things such as discipline, respect, integrity, and character. Failures and successes have helped me to appreciate things I once took for granted. There are two things that must be and are being fostered in the processing of our lives. That is simply how we think and what we speak. Both are the most powerful sources of our human existence.

Proverbs 18:21 states *"Death and life are in the power of the tongue"*. The reason that this and many other scriptures convey this thought is because God has given us the ability to create an environment using nothing but words. Words are powerful and transcending. God used words to create and He has given us from His DNA the ability to do the same. How we use it is another story. How we speak becomes another part of the process we must learn to transition towards positive things in our lives. What we speak and how we speak whether in thought or in audible words is still our speech.

This is the ground where you come to grips with God's existence and your very own. It is the place that you are introduced to God's way of living life. The outcome of this process is determined by whom you allow to sit on the throne of your heart when you face the conflicts in your life and the attitude you choose to carry. How you go through the process is reflective in the outcome. For example, if you are a procrastinator then your process is surely to last much longer than someone who confronts challenges immediately. If you are someone who has issues of anger then things will continue to arise in your life that will challenge you to control and channel your anger until humility finds the greater ground of your temperament. You may be afraid of success because you fear failure. You will never rise to the level you desire by allowing fear to grip who you are. You may sabotage what is good because there is a part of you that feels like you don't deserve it. Your process will be filled with opportunities to teach you to forgive yourself and overcome fear. Healing, forgiveness, humility, courage, faith, empowerment, education, change and trust are all a part of the process.

The real kicker is that none of our lives have been presented to us in a script, so we have no idea of what will come our way from one day to the next. Each and every day is filled with choices. From the time we wake up in the morning we are presented with a choice: to either get out of bed or stay in the bed; to go to work or to stay home; to go to school or drop out; to fight, or to walk away; to drink or not to drink; to enter a relationship or not to enter the relationship. Even the path we drive to work is a choice. So when we commence our daily routine we live out the day answering the questions of choice. Many of the choices we make are reflective of our character which also serves as a barometer of our progress or lack thereof.

Process is God's way of getting us to His desired outcome and it is a method filled with challenges and conflicts, successes and joy. Happiness and sadness, joy and pain, good times and frustrations, love and heartaches. Some of the people God has chosen to do some of the most monumental things in human history were people who spent years and much of their lives within a process that was spent preparing them for the ultimate purpose of their life. Moses was 80 years old when he received his assignment to lead the children of Israel from bondage out of Egypt. Jesus was 30 when he began a public ministry that would last a total of three years, but would revolutionize world religion and forever change human perspective of God. Process is not to be avoided but rather embraced. If you are in a process that is not moving at the pace you are looking for, seek patience rather than a quick escape. If you prepare a meal and in haste take what you have prepared out of the oven too soon, the result can be disastrous. Meals hastily prepared end up making people sick and can cause them to be reluctant to receive something you cook again.

In the book of James it says "My brethren count it all joy when you fall into various temptations knowing that the testing of your faith produces patience but let patience have her perfect work that you may be perfect and entire wanting nothing" (James 1:1 NKJV).

In the scripture God addresses His process of development. "But let patience have her perfect work that you may be perfect and entire wanting nothing". The word *"perfect"* actually suggests maturity or to mature. The word *"entire"* which means complete and the word *"wanting"* is properly translated as lacking. So the full expression of the last thought reads, *"Let patience have her complete work so that you may be mature and complete, lacking nothing".* This introduces God's purpose for your life by introducing you into His process. Simply put, God wants you to be mature and complete. This is part of His restoration process to mature you and complete you. When I have looked upon the failures and disappointments in my lifetime I have often wondered, what was the purpose of those experiences. As I have thought and reflected on them I have come to realize that God wastes nothing. Even what I have messed up in my life somehow God has used to serve a greater purpose. Meaning, that even the mistakes you and I make often are woven within a process to mature us to a point that makes our experiences invaluable to someone else. Don't run from God's process for your life, but rather embrace it. It will ultimately help you and bless someone else.

CHAPTER TWO

THE FALL

Since the outcome of things we want in life is desirable, the process can be very challenging. *"Count it all joy when you fall"* **(James 1:1NKJV)...** Who really wants to fall or fail?

I have often examined and searched for the cause of my past mistakes and failures, perhaps you have done the same. Like a broken record or a radio station that had only one song in its catalog, I played my failures over and over again in my head. Each time the song ended I felt worse than I did when I began playing it. I don't believe that anyone can do anything worse to a person who has fallen than what they can do to themselves mentally. What is done most of the time is that we cover up the fact that we hurt internally and are in anguish over our shortcomings. But we don't feel comfortable typically allowing others to see it, because we don't want them to perceive that we are weak and feeling vulnerable. In other words, we don't feel at ease to allow someone else to know that we are human. We then develop a disguise or mask to hide our flaw(s). Shame is a hard taskmaster. Often the greater the position we hold in our careers or other circles including church, the more cleaver the mask we wear. As the old commercial put it "never let em see you sweat," or as Lawrence Dunbar's poem is so appropriate, "we wear the mask".

Condemnation is to a person who has a conscience of morality very overwhelming when confronted by their failure. In other words you beat yourself up worse than the people who look to inflict condemning judgments against you. But understand that condemnation is not what God puts upon us, it is what we place upon ourselves. His way of gaining our attention is through the arousing of our conscience through His penetrating yet graceful words.

For example, the story of the woman caught in adultery as expressed in John 8:2-12 has two sides that address this thought. The nature of the story is evidenced by these compelling facts. One, the woman was caught in the act of adultery, which merely speaks to the fact that she fell and everyone knew about it. Secondly, the man is never brought to the forefront with the woman, just her alone isolated to face the ridicule, judgment, and sentencing of the people. It's the nature of Satan and sin and illicit living to attract you with a false sense of security through secrecy. When it is finished with you, it destroys you with exploitation and shame and ultimately death of some type. What must be honestly looked upon is the fact that secrecy is where the sin gets its strength. The greater the secret becomes the more powerful the sin becomes. And the greater the energy and effort must be afforded to the cause to keep it a secret thus rendering the person concealing it a prisoner of the cause. If sin is the egg then secrecy is the incubator.

Herein lays the issue with many believers of Christ. What is often missed is that you can be saved but not delivered, called but flawed, chosen but inept. Please do not make the assumption that sin merely is limited to the pews. Clearly recent history has shown us that sin can reach the greater points of the church leaving no stone or saint unturned. Worldly media has made it a point to expose it and quite frankly much of the church has aided in the process of exploitation. From the door post to the pulpit, from the crack house to the white house no one is immune from sin's touch. The unfortunate problem is that we don't expect it to touch the priest. We will examine this fact, as we look closer in chapter three.

The Bible clearly makes it known that the woman is "caught" in the act of adultery. However what it does not address is how long the affair was happening before she was caught. What led to the affair and how long was it entertained before it was acted out? Was it a one-time experience or did she struggle from a type of sexual addiction brought on by shame? Was she a victim of abuse or neglect from her husband, family, or other people? Was she caught in a web of deceit with the man she found herself involved with? What was she promised? Where did she think her experiences would take her? Sin is always entertained before it is acted out. The illusion is that it will not get out of control or become destructive as one may think.

Think about when you found yourself caught in something that you wished you could get out of. Trouble is always easier to get into than to get out of. This is the result of a fallen world. You may be reading this right now struggling to find a way out of a circumstance or debilitating relationship. Thankfully God always provides a way out

"Therefore let him who thinks he stands take heed lest he falls. No temptation has over-taken you except such as is common to man; but God is faithful, who will not allow you to be tempted beyond what you are able, but with the temptation will also make the way of escape, that you may be able to bear it" **(I Corinthians 10:12-13NKJV).**

But the question is, are you willing to take the way God is providing or will you allow your pride to keep you captive to the circum-stances you find yourself in? God's way always ends with healing and restoration. Whenever we give into sin the result always ends in death and humiliation.

We are just examining this woman in an adulterous relationship, but sin addresses all forms of addictions. From alcohol to drugs to lying, yes lying. Some people are habitual liars and it is just as much a sin as adultery, steal-ing, or killing. What you must realize is that you didn't just appear in the sinful act. There were moments, hours, days, and months or even years of premeditation involved. Sin is always incubated before it is hatched. You wrestled before you gave in to the sin.

"Each one is tempted when he is drawn away of his own desires and enticed. Then, when desire has conceived, it gives birth to sin; and sin, when it is full-grown, brings forth death" **(James 1:14-15NKJV).**

Remember it's not a sin to be tempted it's a sin to yield. You and I can do nothing about being tempted but we can do something about yielding through Christ's help. Resistance is a power that God gives us if we ask. *"Lead us not into temptation but deliver us from the evil one"* (Matthew 6:13NKJV).

Let us suppose that the woman had been involved in the affair for some time. Perhaps she had internally wanted to break off the affair but her flesh was out of control. While she convinced herself she was in control by saying "this is the last time". She enjoyed the sin as much as she hated it. Anyone who really does love God and desires to live for Him can and are many times caught in this vicious dilemma. The inherent struggle, sin's taste is sweet, but its effects are deadly. By the time we read of her plight the fruit was manifested on the tree. But how long did the tree exist? Jesus states that *"a good tree cannot bear bad fruit and a bad tree cannot bear good fruit"* (Matthew 7:18NKJV). What we tend to react to most of the time is the fruit evidenced on our trees.

Getting upset and throwing an apple far away after plucking it from the tree will not change the fact that it's an apple tree nor will it stop the apples from growing back after one or all have been plucked. This is why simply telling someone, what he or she can or cannot wear or do to be considered "acceptable" in the church or other places, does nothing to change the heart of the person. They merely find someplace else to wear it or do it. You are merely plucking fruit off the branches.

Ostracizing someone from the church because of fruit on their tree will not change the person nor win the person to Christ. Our responsibility is to share the truth (God's word and not ours) and allow the Holy Spirit to do His Job. Trust me, He has much greater experience at turning someone's life around than you or I do. And He has been doing it much longer than we have. Regulating someone's actions does not regulate his or her heart. Of course this is not to suggest that we live without guidelines or principles. However, it does mean that you and I will never change a person by merely controlling their actions. This is why the correctional institutions produce so many repeat offenders and so many returns to prison. The system is not set up for true rehabilitation but rather incarceration. It is designed to control actions and not change hearts. It is only when one's heart is changed that the outcome is changed.

Instead of us just being master fruit inspectors, we should seek to become master root inspectors. How you kill a bad tree is by attacking and killing its roots. This is very significant because the roots do not thrive above ground. They live underneath the dirt where no one can see them. You know it's there but no one really pays much attention to it because the roots do not thrive above ground. No one really pays much attention to it because it's not obvious to us, very much like the sin that can enthrone our lives. By the time we observe people, we have made our assessments based on their fruits. If a person has bad fruit on their tree then we should pray and ask God to help us to discern the roots so we can encourage them towards healing. Rather than just reacting to the fruit, pray that God will address their roots. And remember, you have roots, too. Tucked underneath the dirt of your life, is a place, which symbolizes the feeding ground that makes your roots thrive and the place that either nurtures you to strong character or to possess spiritual fortitude. Or, it is a place that feeds the addictive cravings of your weakness that will undermine all that is good in your life. Dirt can make bad trees grow or good trees grow. The dirt doesn't define the tree, the roots do. The dirt merely helps the tree survive. In other words the environment that covers the roots will either help the roots grow or help them die. What serves as dirt in your life or better yet, who serves as dirt in your life? You may be reading this and find yourself with bad roots surrounded by good dirt, like in a good church or thriving ministry. I assure you that no matter how good your surroundings, if you do not address the roots of your life you will produce bad fruit.

How many people that are mere servants in church or Pastors in pulpits have the appearance of having good roots, but continue to produce bad fruit. This is a real epidemic in our congregations and has undermined much of our witness and effectiveness in our communities. Please understand that we should not give the illusion that everyone in our churches is suffering from bad roots. Rather it is only to suggest that it is a real issue that needs to be examined. By the same token you can have good roots and be in the midst of bad dirt. If you do not change the soil, the roots can ultimately die. So it then stands to reason if you have bad roots and remain in bad soil you have little or no chance of surviving. The good news is that the Lord can give you the transplant you need to ensure your roots become healthy and whole.

The woman in our text of John 8 is isolated, confronted and exploited at the same time. When sin is done with you it will leave you isolated which is where Satan wanted you in the first place without accountability and security. There are countless wounded and stranded believers that find themselves, feeling completely alone, here left to deal with their addictions. While we have brought out the woman's obvious issue, there are numerous addictions, which are brought on through shame. Sexual addiction, alcohol, drugs, spending, lying, stealing, and many others. No one is an island to himself or herself, but pride and shame will have you shipwrecked on an island left to deal with your choices often alone searching for a way to survive; thus rendering you ineffective for God's purpose and plan. God's plan in addressing the weakness of man has always been through accountability.

"Two are better than one, because they have a good reward for their labor. For if they fall one will lift up his companion. But woe to him who is alone when he falls, for he has no one to help him up" **(Ecclesiastes 4:9-10NKJV).**

The one with no accountability is sure to fall while the one with someone to keep them accountable has the assurance of covering if they should fall. To the person overwhelmed with sinful habits of addictions, "account-ability" can be uncomfortable and seem like a bad word. But the lack of accountability also violates the principle of respect, which we will address in Chapter four. *"Where there is no counsel, the people fall, but in the multitude of counselors there is safety"* (Proverbs 11:14NKJV).

The woman isolated and exploited by the people receives the awesome gift of mercy (which prevented her from getting what she deserved), as well as grace (which is what she received that she didn't deserve according to the law). The intervention of Jesus brings out two sides to this story. But first consider the fact that the son of God (someone in the flesh) became the instrument of intervention to lift the woman up. God always prefers to use people to deliver His people. Why not be that instrument in your world.

The first side which is widely taught and preached and most obvious, is Jesus' statement to the people. "He who is without sin among you, let him throw a stone at her first". This statement (along with the writing on the ground) brings immediate conviction to the people standing as judge, jury, and executioners. We are not told what he wrote on the ground, which of course leaves it open for speculation.

However, I'd like to think that possibly he began to simply write down the sins of life: pride, lying, stealing, killing, covetousness, fornication, idolatry, and the list continues. One, if not more, finding the heart of those standing in judgment over the woman. The oldest left first, in order, until the youngest followed soon after. Perhaps some of the men were angry because secretly they desired her and were not able to engage in the activity themselves. After all, the man was not facing death for the deed, she was. Upon hearing Jesus' words and perhaps reading what he wrote on the ground, the older, I am sure looked over the years of sinful failures that were never brought out in the same way as this woman's sin was exposed.

Regardless of whatever their personal conviction was, the point is no one was willing nor wanting their personal sins exposed or exploited. Many probably walked away still in bondage to whatever their sin was. Jesus never discussed what his or her personal sins were in front of everyone else. No one likes to have their weaknesses exploited so why do we tend to find opportunity to exploit others. As a good Pastor of mine once said, "we like to maximize others' imperfections, while minimizing our own". Indeed somehow seeing someone else's faults can sometimes make us not feel so bad about our own. Thus taking out the sense of urgency to deal with our own sin and unbeknown to us, keeping us further entrapped in our prison. Just as the people walked off not wanting their sins exposed, no one else today enjoys feeling exploited. The point of Jesus' actions were obviously to make the people look at themselves. That is a tall order in today's society and has been an age-less issue since the original fall of Adam and Eve. It's always easier to look at the faults of others rather than deal with your own faults and struggles. That has been an unmistakable reality as recent exposures of national church leadership misconducts and indiscretions have been made public knowledge. While many of those who have been sensitive to this subject understand the importance of prayer over criticism, many others seized the opportunity to become a part of the "stoning" party. While I certainly do not support nor advocate wrong in the church and in church leadership, I do realize that we really don't have room to judge someone to the level of exploitation and condemnation. If God dealt with us merely on the issues and offences we have done towards Him, in our thoughts alone, we would all be in a world of trouble. You may be saying I haven't done anything to anyone or with anyone. I have just kept my thoughts to myself. The Bible assures us that the heart is not a place of hid-ing unto God. You may cover it from people, but it is an open book to Him whether it is filled with passion and love for Him and His creation, or whether it is darkened and hardened by deceit, lust, and abominable thoughts.

The other side of this story was for the woman. This side is not often taught or examined; however, consider with me the following thought: Jesus addressed the people to remove them from her presence because they served as tormentors to her guilt. He never said anything to her until he removed them from her presence. Why? Perhaps because she would have been consumed by their presence and distracted from hearing his words and focusing on his presence. Their words would have had a stronger grip on her than his words. God doesn't shout to get our attention. He speaks with a still small voice. His ways are strong, yet gentle.

In my experiences, I have heard so many people who are just beginning their lives again in church or even those who have attended church for years, ask the same question that all of us ask at some point. How do you learn how to hear God's voice? My response to that question is quite simple. I equate learning God's voice to the same concept of any relationship. When you are first meeting someone it takes time to be able to recognize their voice when they call. For example, when someone you have first met calls you on the telephone or you call them the call is met by a greeting of, "Hi John, this is..." The need to identify who is calling is based on the reality that the experience with this person is extremely limited and untested. After time has been spent talking with this person over days, weeks, or months on a consistent basis, the need to identify who is calling suddenly seems unnecessary. This is because there has been enough dialog and connection to recognize them apart from anyone else. So my answer to the question of how to hear God's voice is quite simple. Pray (which is merely a spiritual form of communication) and pour out your heart to God and then sit quietly to hear the voice begin to speak in your heart.

Keep in mind that when He speaks, His words will always match the character of His word. People often look for God to speak loudly through thunderous circumstances or tragic events and indeed He may choose to utilize that approach. However, He prefers to use a peaceful whisper, a gentle or strong word, but not a shout. To shout at someone can signify a situation that is getting out of your control. We shout to gain the control back. God is never out of control so why should He have to shout to gain our attention.

Jesus once spoke that "the doorkeeper (Christ) opens, and the sheep hear his voice; and he calls his own by name and leads them out" (John 10:3NKJV).

God never wants anyone else to have a greater influence in your life than Him. So, He will do whatever is necessary to move or remove the distractions and destructor from your life so you can hear Him clearly and serve Him better. Remember, God is jealous of anything or anyone that has a stronger influence in your life than He does. If you have ever fallen in love with someone, you can probably relate to that feeling. There is always a need to feel that your loved one is more influenced by your voice than another man or woman. You were created for His glory, not yours nor anyone else's. So it is an erroneous notion to assume that God will give you the very best He has to offer your life when you give Him nothing or very little of your life. He can and will sustain you out of His love and your need but not give you abundance out of your desires and wants. The relationship that suddenly went bad may have been for the purpose of drawing you closer. Perhaps it was not a healthy association and caused you to be disillusioned by what is right and pure before Him. God will remove it if it means you getting closer to Him and becoming more like Him. It is much better to lose a temporary unhealthy relationship than an eternal great one. He loves you that much. You may be trying to hold onto something or someone that God has rejected as being non-beneficial to your life. Remember God is not interested in you failing; He is interested in you overcoming.

The purpose from the woman's perspective was to see that she was not an isolated case and no matter how much the people were attempting to destroy her by making her feel isolated and condemned, everyone was guilty. Imagine that, Jesus wanted her to see everyone's guilt without telling what everyone did. My friend, take courage and know that no matter how isolated and alone you may feel at this moment, you are not alone. No matter what type of sin you may have stumbled into there is someone who has or is or will go through the same things you have. This is most liberating to me because no matter how much I have preached and heard other Pastors or ministers preach or teach and believers quote, the Apostle Paul stated *"All have sinned and fallen short of the glory of God"* (Romans 3:23NKJV). We still treat people like the woman caught in adultery. What is it in us that seeks to destroy others that have some obvious level of guilt in their life or something we consider heinous? What makes us feel that our faults are somehow less significant than theirs, so we feel we should become judge over them? We must be willing to be honest with God and ourselves and remember that He is aware at all times. So indeed, honesty is the best policy. Honesty beginning with you is being truthful with yourself. And what God desires is truth so that we can be liberated. David vividly articulated this point, *"Behold, You desire truth in the inward parts"* (Psalm 51:6NKJV).

Sin's Subtleness

From the beginning, I never saw myself as anyone who would fall because of my relationship with God and often I felt justified by the position I held in church. In my mind it was never an issue of whether or not I loved God. I loved Him but I didn't love myself. So was my love for God what it should be? *Genesis 3:1 says that the serpent was more cunning than any other beast of the field.* His approach to Eve was through observation before communication. What you must realize is that Satan is an observer, he is not omnipresent, but he does observe. He studies our weaknesses and our appetites. He doesn't approach you with anything that is not an enticement to your flesh. He presents to you exactly what your flesh or mind craves or is stimulated by to allure you.

His initial approach is not a full-blown explosion of the sin, but rather a small seed of enticement to grasp your attention. The idea here that he has is not to give you an immediate destruction, but rather a slow and painful death. The appearance seems harmless in the beginning. When I accepted Christ at the age of 19 and received my calling, I was under the impression that I was somehow immediately translated to a level of spiritual invincibility. Talk about being disillusioned. In becoming saved I received Christ as my Savior; however, I hadn't learned to make him Lord. In the Greek the word lord means "controller". What a distinctive spin that puts on the word. Does He have complete control over everything in your life? That means your actions, thoughts and ways. It suggests that a complete surrender has taken place, a transfer of authority and power. It means that we come off the throne of our heart and allow Christ to take our place. The throne of a man's heart is made for only one person to sit and God won't share it. Either He sits on it, we sit on it, or someone else sits on it. After all, He is worthy of it since He took our place on the cross.

Unaware that as heaven rejoiced over my decision to follow God, Satan salivated at the chance to undo what God was doing and going to do. What we often don't understand is that in heaven there is a picture that flows from the heart and mind of God that shows you in your matured state of purpose. What a beautiful picture it is. Heaven is filled with expectation for you to fulfill your purpose here on earth. But as the angels are witness to the plan of God for your life, Satan is also an observer and witness of that picture. This explains why he is so determined to destroy the seed of your life before it can blossom into the tree God intended it to become.

Just look at Job and take note of Satan's observation. *"Now there was a day when the sons of God came to present themselves before the Lord, and Satan also came among them. And the Lord said to Satan, "From where do you come?" So Satan answered the Lord and said, "From going to and fro on the earth, and from walking back and forth on it". Then the Lord said to Satan, "Have you considered My servant Job, that there is none like him on the earth, a blameless and upright man, one who fears God and shuns evil?" So Satan answered the Lord and said, "Does Job fear God for nothing? Have you not made a hedge around him, around his household, and around all that he has on every side? You have blessed the work of his hands and the possessions have increased in the land. But now stretch out your hand and touch all that he has, and he will* *surely curse You to Your face!" And the Lord said to Satan, "Behold, all that he has is in your power; only do not lay a hand on his person." So Satan went out from the presence of the Lord"* (Job 1:6-12NKJV).

So while God is committed to helping you become everything He has created you to be by utilizing all means at His disposal. More significantly, Gods wants to illuminate and activate what He has placed in you to become. Be assured that Satan is equally committed to perverting and undermining everything God has planned for your life. First, he will use ignorance by keeping you blind and deaf to the truth of God's will, word, purpose, and power. Secondly, disillusioned by showing and convincing you great material things are the greatest expression of success and fulfillment. And finally, through disobedience by convincing you to give heed to the desires of your flesh and focus all of your attention and efforts on self. However, since we serve an omniscient (all knowing) God He will use whatever Satan has planned to destroy us with to in turn mature us to righteousness. But the key is that we must be willing to allow God to do it. That's where His lordship in your life comes to play. And keep in mind that, *"All things work together for our good to those who love God and are called according to His purpose"* (Romans 8:28 NKJV).

Unaware of how these things worked in the spiritual realm of existence, I found myself within the first two years of ministry confronted by the forbidden fruit of my garden. I caught a glimpse of something at 21 years of age that captivated my curious mind. As a teenager, I was probably like most young boys who find themselves discovering their bodily sensations. But I was not an out of control person. I was not promiscuous, which would have been considered unacceptable by the boys in the locker room. Mainly, I was quiet, shy and alone. However, at age 21, I caught a glimpse of an older woman who revealed to me something that captivated my mind. While I never physically touched her body nor was there ever a communication shared on what she was revealing, it began a spiraling cycle that would plague and destroy everything good and pure in my life for the next 20 years. The one image that she shared of her body part was the small seed that would grow into a tree of destruction. Song of Solomon 2:15 states, "The small foxes spoil the vines". That image she shared that was forbidden, was all it took. My imagination took over and in time because I did not physically touch her, I touched her over and over again in my mind. Eventually I found myself looking for the image in other women in pornographic magazines. The irony of it was that I was "saved" and called to preach, but I couldn't tell anyone where my struggle lied. It was a desire to experience the untouchable in my head. Like Satan taking Christ to the peak of a mountain and showing Him all the kingdoms of the world (Matthew 4:8). Or God taking Moses to the edge of the Promised Land and showing it all to him, but Moses not being able to cross over. I played with this perverted image in my head and looked to foster it through another woman's body. Magazine after magazine, I searched (undercover of course) but could never seem to find the satisfaction I searched for so desperately. Magazines soon turned to videos looking to appease my sense of curiosity and blossoming perversion. The women I looked upon ceased to be people who may have suffered some type of emotional pains in their lives that led them down a path to bare the sacred parts of their bodies. They were just mere images to me. They were objects of illusive lustful images that spoke to my curiosity. I soon married and two years later my son arrived. Thinking that it would somehow douse the flame that seemed to burn in my memory, layer upon layer I added to my life dirt, hoping to smother the kindled image or root that began so innocently.

Please understand that one of Satan's greatest joys is to pervert things that God makes pure. But no matter what I did to try to live a "normal saved" life, I found that the image was turning into a stronghold. I was committed to preach the word of God. I had an image to uphold. A minister, a husband, a father, but no one could know my secret. I mean God forbid anyone see that I was human with flaws and weaknesses like everyone else. Or perhaps that I'd present myself damaged to the church of righteous believers. The pressure of being super human and super righteous seemed to only fuel my buried secret.

The years rolled by as I perfected my gift of preaching. I knew I had to be articulate and wise so that people would feel that I had things together. Boy was I choking with pride. Soon my marriage was violated with infidelity, while I preached the gospel. The more the people seemed to respond positively to the sermons I preached the more it seemed to fuel this desire to stay up on top of things. But the problem was that the same thing I preached against, I was becoming. My love for God was soon equaled by my push for the sin I indulged. You see, when we refuse to address the sin that so easily besets us it soon becomes an interwoven part of our existence and character. Suddenly peace flees us and the level of closeness we once enjoyed with God fades into a memory. We long for that closeness, but feel unworthy of what we want with God. We feel dirty and now we hide ourselves. Rather than running to God, we run from Him. My friend it's time to stop running from Him and run to Him.

The illusion was that somehow I could handle or overcome anything, without anyone knowing, simply because I trusted no one. Everyone was suspect, but the hard question was could I be trusted.

The Bible clearly outlines the fact that hell is a place of torments. And when you are in a place of addictive struggle it can feel as though you have landed in hell. So the last thing anyone needs is to have others come and serve as the instrument of torments. I told God on one occasion that I did not want to be an instrument of destruction any longer, but make me to be an instrument of healing. Our prayer ought to be that the Lord helps us to become instruments of righteousness and healing for people, which is His greatest commodity.

I have found myself in 23 years of service for God in both positions as the accuser and the guilty. It was much easier for me to operate as an accuser than the guilty. The accuser is motivated through pride and denial. Their pride tends to suggests that somehow they are better than the person they are judging.

Somehow if they condemn someone else it helps justify their own conscience and keeps them from addressing their own personal faults. Their denial suggests that somehow their sin isn't as bad as the other sin they are judging. Therein lays a great problem amongst many believers. Sin rating, whenever we rate sin, we give a type of credence to sin that might suggest that certain forms may be more tolerable than others. While all sins may have varying consequences, all sin is wrong in the eyes of God. We have no right to rate sin, when all sin is an offense to God. Simple disobedience to God is a sin. If God told you to do something like forgive someone you don't want to forgive and you don't' do it that is a sin. James 4:17 states, *"to him who knows to do good and does not do it, to him it is sin"*. Don't be caught by the subtlety of sin, recognize and call it for what it is and allow God's light of truth to eradicate it from your life. As challenging as that may sound, it is the first step to healthy living.

Interesting Story

It wasn't until I found myself in the position of Pastor 20 years later that God was about to bring my tormenting secret to a head. I was Pastor to a people who enjoyed the articulate teaching of a man who was secretly tainted.

As much as I personally anguished over the sin that seemed to so easily trouble my life. I was in fear of being exposed. I had convinced myself that I had the sin in my life under control when in all reality, it had me under control. I feared being exposed; however, in truth, I had lost my fear of God. My friend reverent fear of God is the grounding tool that keeps us humble before God. When you lose your fear for God and the things of God, destruction is never far behind. *"The fear of the Lord is the beginning of knowledge, but fools despise wisdom and instruction"* (Proverbs 1:7 NKJV).

I never realized how much immodesty had strangled all of the good in my life until the destructive force of my actions became sur-real. I continued to preach with great passion and fervor. I took such self-satisfaction in the fact that the ministry had "strong" word. What I was failing to realize was that the strength of the word is not to be absent of the strength of character. I had such a false sense of humility because I would allow others to come and do things in the ministry many times without any true accountability. I had come under such self-condemnation that bringing correction where it was needed and necessary was a mute-point. The ministry became crippled because of a lack of strong leadership, under girded by iniquity (supported by sin). What one must realize is that iniquity (which is hidden sins) and integrity cannot co-exist. When a person struggles with an addiction of any kind, the pending result that undermines righteousness is compromise. I wrestled and often anguished with God, asking why the ministry would not grow. I examined everything possible in the church regarding the reason of our lack of community impact and appeal for membership growth. After all, I felt I had something to prove to all the nay-sayers who perceived God did not call our church to exist. I found myself relying on my personal "know how" and inner strength. I would call it persevering for righteousness sake. But in truth, I was persevering for my own sake. God had long been put on the backside of the desert, which is where I belonged. I sat on the throne of my own heart and allowed my self-righteousness to dictate the path I was journeying.

Unintentionally, I had created a plan and asked God to jump on board and bless it. Have you found yourself completely frustrated because things have not gone the way you planned? Perhaps you should examine if the steps you have chosen to take are the steps you laid out or the steps God has laid out for you.

Unknown to my congregation I often came in the church during normal business hours when no one was around falling on my face at the altar in torment and tears. I begged God to help me to overcome my greatest weakness. It managed after 20 years to destroy everything good and pure in my life. My family suffered. My first marriage destroyed. My children suffered and now my church was suffering. I somehow convinced myself that everything would be fine every time God would move in our worship services. Every time God would use me to bring such an intense message that found people rushing to the altar for prayer, salvation or being healed, I somehow felt that I was alright. God was about to remind me that He once used a donkey (and I am being nice by saying donkey) to perform His will. Isn't it amazing how quickly we can forget that we need God more than He needs us? Don't ever let your apparent success in life, business, career or ministry, somehow dismiss the fact that God requires of your character as much as He does your availability. If He will use a donkey to give a word if necessary, or use rocks to verbalize His praises, then where does that leave us?

Let me preach or teach the hell out of the church, but in reality, it needed to be taught out of me. Altar calls, people filled, salvation ministered, and many saved. Hospital visitations and people were actually healed. Yet, the church could not grow; it would not grow.

The vision was clearly defined and articulated and motto and core values presented in great fashion, yet behind me laid a path of unmentionable destruction brought on by the sinful fruit that fell from my tree. Sunday highs were followed by Monday lows. As spiritually uplifted as I would get on Sunday mornings, it would be quickly brought low by Monday's reality. All of this was coming to a head. The tragic aspect of what I have just shared was that it was not the first time a church I Pastored suffered because of my unresolved sin. This was my second opportunity to assume such a great and awesome task. It was the second time that it ended with the same demise. I cannot begin to express to you the level of humiliation and embarrassment I felt and brought upon my family and church family. If anyone felt that someone needed to be taken out and stoned to death, it was certainly me. What do you do with a Pastor that is as flawed as I was and trying to minister to flawed people? What avenues does he have to address his personal challenges? God would only allow this act of defiant disobedience to take place for so long. In my heart I loved God, but inwardly, I struggled to obey Him.

Finally, at a most inopportune moment, in the most humiliating way God exposed my secret. The sudden reality hit me like the woman caught in adultery. I scrambled to find cover, but there was none to be found. His light invaded my darkness and suddenly there I was naked before Him and those close to me. Suddenly the reality of 20 years came crashing like a plane out of the sky and I could do nothing, but brace for impact. When I hit the ground I can remember nothing, but being completely and helplessly shattered. I cried and sobbed for weeks and could not seem to get myself together. I could find no comfort. Nothing my ex-spouse would do could ease the earth shattering experience I was feeling. After all she did not know what I was about to confess to her.

My transparency here is to reach out to you who may be reading this and remind you that no matter what you do, your sins do affect people close to you. I found no comfort in anything I would do or anything anyone would say. God's anger was kindled and I had taken His grace for granted. God was not requiring, "I'm sorry," He was requiring repentance (which simply means to stop and turn around). I found no strength to see anything critical of anyone but myself. "I failed God," was all I could seem to muster the strength to say. I told my spouse of that time, that I was tired and I continued to sob uncontrollably. I suddenly saw the ministry closing and my marriage folding before my eyes. It wasn't just the indiscretion that I faced, it was 20 years of sin that I was being forced to deal with. The indiscretion was the fruit, God was dealing with the root and it was about to be exposed to me once and for all. As much emotional pain that I was forced to deal with I was able to put things into perspective. I would not dare blame God or anyone else for where I found myself. What a tremendous mistake we make when we seek to blame others instead of taking responsibility for our own actions. God was taking back what rightfully belonged to Him in the first place, my life. I took a brief sabbatical from the church, which would ultimately close, to go and spend time with my spouse at that time. We took a trip to New Jersey to visit with my father and to deal with the experience that was suddenly upon us. And unwary to me I was about to receive my first message from God, about what was happening.

Suicide Attempt

While sitting between services in a room at the church my dad serves in, someone came in and began sharing a story that took place over the course of the previous weekend. The woman shared the story of a man who the day prior attempted to commit suicide at a local mall. Fed up and hopeless from his circumstances his agenda was to leap from a 3 story-parking garage and fall to his death. It was apparent that God had a different plan. Upon leaping to what he considered his final act in life, he only managed to land upon the grass lawn below, but not before nearly missing a woman on the way down. His selfish actions resulted in him merely shattering the bones in his body and upsetting the innocent woman passing by. His inability to cope with the issues in his life and feelings of hopelessness caused him to create more devastating circumstances rather than eliminating them. He wanted to end his life and instead he just complicated it more. Have you ever felt like your decisions have put you into a hole deeper than the one you found yourself in before? While I am sure he never intended to hurt anyone but himself, his actions caused tremendous emotional and psychological trauma to the woman passing by. Whenever we choose to do things that serve our own interests without consideration of others, the outcome can be equally destructive to others' lives around us. What you must realize is that all sin is selfish. Sin is based on one person, "Me". It's all about what makes us feel good and what we want and takes no consideration towards how anyone else feels. Most believers in Christ see suicide as the last sinful act that can be committed by anyone. Yet, there is a symbolism of suicide anytime we continue a path that has a destructive outcome, *"The wages (payment or outcome) of sin is death, but the gift of God is eternal life"* (Romans 6:23NKJV).

The outcome of the man's suicide attempt was anything but successful because the jump he made was not high enough to kill him, but high enough to break him. This is what the Lord shared with me concerning my experience. How befitting it was as this revelation was shown to me about my life and current circumstances. It seemed to fit me like a glove. I was experiencing for the first time, true brokenness and it was just what I needed to begin the recovery and restoration process. You cannot be completely utilized by God without true brokenness. Humility in its purest form is adored by God. If you are trying to figure out what really moves the heart of God, nothing speaks sincerity like brokenness. It's not fashionable, in fact, it's quite painful, but it's the greatest form of liberation you can experience when you come to the place of realizing you have nothing else to offer. All resources completely depleted and relationships unreliable, it is the sobering reality of human failure and spiritual unrighteousness. It cannot be cloaked or masked by religion or any expression that draws deception towards God. True brokenness brings you to grips with how far you have drifted away from the love and righteousness of God. Suddenly nothing else matters but the complete surrendering desire to please God and the willingness to honor Him. My desires and tastes for sin left me like yesterday's sunshine. I couldn't find a trace of it. Brokenness is the reckoning process that agrees with God's assertion that all our righteousness are like filthy rags (Isaiah 64:6NKJV).

Until the process of brokenness takes place, you can tend to feel as though you cannot find God in a way you may have experienced Him at one point in your life. However, in all reality, it is a fact that sin does separate us from God. It's not that God has drifted from your life my friend, but rather that you may have drifted from Him. God is the purest expression and form of love and love is the greatest manifestation of selflessness. Sin and addiction on the other hand are the greatest form of selfishness and pride. It only thinks of itself and seeks to gratify itself at the expense of others. Love gives of itself and continues to give without end. You and I can never fully exhaust God's love. His love endures throughout all generations. Out of His bosom of love for us, He allows us to become broken that we may be drawn closer to Him. When you are not broken before Him, obedience is just an act of religious obligation under the law. When you have been broken obedience becomes an act of love.

"Confess your trespasses (faults) to one another, and pray for one another, that you may be healed" (James 5:16 NKJV).

Confessing your sins is practical and sound advice, but it has a qualifying tone to the scripture. In principle we should be able to go to anyone in the fellowship of friends and believers to bare our weaknesses with the hope of receiving spiritual and emotional guidance, support and unconditional love. Unfortunately, this has posed great issues in many church circles because not everyone is on the same spiritual level that allows for that type of transparency and confession to be expressed. The Apostle Paul once wrote *"if a man is overtaken in any trespass, you who are spiritual restore such a one in a spirit of gentleness, considering yourself lest you also be tempted"* (Galatians 6:1 NKJV). God's desire is for us as believers and followers of His word to mature to a point where we can help others heal from their faults and not crucify them because of their faults. It has amazed me that over the years I taught many lessons, and had countless altar calls, and preached messages that addressed restoration and forgiveness, yet I have found a great famine in many of those same church circles because there was a lack of true forgiveness or restoration.

There was a lot of judgment and harsh criticism and in some cases, ostracizing. I believe holding someone accountable for their actions is necessary and one thing, but shunning someone because of their faults is another. But the faults and weaknesses that are carried by many are not isolated to those outside the church or those just entering the church. Those who serve in the highest office within the church walls have often fallen prey to their weaknesses as well. What is important here is to adjust our perspective of how we view those in high positions.

CHAPTER THREE

THE DOCTOR IS SICK?

The Spirit of the Lord is upon Me, Because He has anointed Me to preach the gospel to the poor; He has sent Me to heal the brokenhearted, to proclaim liberty to the captives and recovery of sight to the blind. To set at liberty those who are oppressed; to proclaim the acceptable year of the Lord. Then He closed the book, and gave it back to the attendant and sat down. And the eyes of all who were in the synagogue were fixed on Him. And He began to say to them, "Today this scripture is fulfilled in your hearing". So they all were witness to Him and marveled at the gracious words which proceeded out of His mouth. And they said "is this not Joseph's son?" He said to them "You will

surely say this proverb to Me, "Physician, heal yourself"... (Luke 4:18-23NKJV).

Expectations are something that come with positions of responsibility. Whether the expectations are realistic or not, fair or not, they span a variety of capacities whether it is the President of the United States or the President of the company we work for or the President of the group we are associated with or even the Pastor of the local church. As the saying goes, "with great power, comes great responsibility", and as Jesus said *"For everyone to whom much is given, from him much will be required; and to whom much has been committed, of him they will ask the more"*(Luke 12:48NKJV). Expectations are a product of any given relationship. Whether the relationship is with parents, children, family, or even someone special in your life or perhaps in a working relationship, we always carry expectations when we enter into a relationship. While what we expect can certainly vary, there is always an expectation attached to the relationship. We don't even have to know a person in order to create an expectation. If we look up to someone we may have never met, there is often anticipation associated with our knowledge of that person. What we envisage from people who are deemed great in their respective fields, can be something much different than what we get from them. We even carry expectations of ourselves. Once again, what we expect from relationships may vary from person to person, but there is always expectancy there. The problem comes when our expectations are not met by the person we look towards and the impact that it makes on us. A failed belief can last for days, months, years and sometimes over a lifetime. So what is it that we need to overcome failed expectations? We need perspective because our view of people and/or ourselves can become significantly altered. Due to failed anticipation we are often left with the challenge of gaining a perspective that will help us overcome our disappointment.

One of the areas I was most disappointed by over the years had very little to do with people that I knew or was associated with. My greatest hurdle was myself. I have struggled with failed expectations since my days in high school. My parents and family can attest to the fact that my childhood ambition in life was to become an airline pilot. I grew up in Los Angeles and the first house I was old enough to remember living in was under the final flight path of the Los Angeles International Airport. While a lot of people could have been significantly bothered by the noise of the engines flying overhead, I was in 7th heaven watching and listening to them. As a child I fell in love with airplanes. I would watch them and study them as they flew over-head with landing gear down and approaching the runway for the landing. I would often ride my bike to the airport and literally hang on the fence just to watch the planes take off and land. My mother worked for a major airline and my father worked in aerospace. We traveled often and I was always fascinated by the thrill of airline travel. In those days airline travel was still fun and exciting. There was no charge for checked baggage, and carry-on luggage. There weren't any charges for using the pillows and blankets, and the meals on the flights were something you could look forward to without being charged. But what I remember most was the fascination I had watching the pilots walk down the jet way before the passengers, as they were preparing their preflight checks for the upcoming journey. On a few occasions I got the opportunity to go to the cockpit very briefly while the plane was in flight just to look at the pilots and see things from their point of view.

One Saturday as a child, my father came and got my brother and I and took us to a small airport to meet a friend of his who owned a small plane. We flew around the Los Angeles area and ended up flying out to Catalina Island for lunch before heading back to our originating airport. It was an experience I would never forget. As my father put it, "we took off in the air and I never came back down". I had one goal in mind through my experiences and that was to be an airline pilot. I had an expectation for myself as I was growing up. I was going to graduate from high school and attend UCLA to get a degree and move on and get trained to become a pilot. Unfortunately what I lacked was the discipline and focus to make it happen. All I possessed was a dream, but what good is a dream if you don't have any plans and actions to support the dream. It will always remain a dream and nothing more. I found out that if a dream is not followed up by actions the dream can transform into regret.

I was never focused in high school and I came up short of even graduating from high school. At the end of the day I had to get my diploma the hard way, by attending adult education school and I never walked the stage with my class. Attending UCLA was only a desire and nothing more. I only had one option which was to join the Air Force. The only problem was I fooled around so much in school that I couldn't pass the test to join the Air Force. It took five tries at taking the test before I would pass it with a high enough score to enter the service. I spent much of my early adult years sorely disappointed with myself. I had not achieved the expectations I had for myself. I used a variety of excuses for why I did not become the pilot I said I would become. My job in the Air Force was to provide aircraft inspections on emergency evacuation equipment. Every time I would climb into the cockpit of an aircraft to perform an inspection on the equipment it would serve as a painful reminder of where I failed myself. I was supposed to be flying the airplane and not merely inspecting it.

I attempted to go to college and take classes, but somewhere along the line I would not finish the classes I would start. This would become a painful habit in my life for years to come. Starting things and not finishing them. Have you ever been in that place before? It is so important that whatever you may start in your life, have the fortitude to complete it. Regret is very difficult to live with and whenever we don't finish what we begin that is typically the feeling we are left with.

Ecclesiastes 9:10 puts it best, *"Whatever your hand finds to do, do it with your might; for there is no work or device or knowledge or wisdom in the grave where you are going"*.

The hard truth was that the failed expectations I had of myself, would lead to several more failed expectations. It was a pattern that began early in my life and was not met with many successes. A failed marriage, struggling churches, damaged relationships. Have you ever felt like you could do nothing but fail? I was amazed that God would allow me to continue to look upon life. But therein lay my hope. There was a reason that I had to go through what I went through and remain here to talk about it. God has a way of taking what we deem as useless and demonstrating that it can still be useful. Please understand my friend that there is nothing that you nor I can do that is so bad that God cannot extract something that is yet beneficial to someone else's life.

Sometimes the failed expectations are not just with us, sometimes they are with God or other people. It is possible to create a probability of God and feel as though He has not met you where you wanted Him to be in your circumstances. Have you ever sat back and watched an opportunity you have prayed for pass onto someone else with little to no apparent effort? When this happens there is often a sentiment that He has somehow failed us and we suddenly become estranged from Him and remove ourselves from the place that we need to be to feel close to Him, like our knees. We stop praying and seeking Him because of our disappointment in what we feel we have not experienced yet. It feels like God has somehow forgotten about us and refuses to grant us what we desire.

At one point I became so disappointed with myself and with God I stopped all together. I stopped praying and I stopped going to church. I was riddled with so much guilt and shame and disgust with myself that I just stopped. Going to church became nothing more than a religious ritual that had very little meaning or impact on me. I had been in ministry so long that I was running through the services in my head from the back row of the church whenever I did attend as though I was orchestrating everything that took place. I found it was becoming easier and easier for me to not attend church, which frightened me. There was a time when I could never imagine missing church, now missing service was not difficult at all. As Pastors, you are in the unique position of being a physician on a spiritual level. I was a wounded and a sick physician and I lacked the capacity to even try to do anything remotely close to serving God or His people.

I was hurt and let down by God, other Pastors and most of all myself. It became easier to just drift away with little or no regard. I felt like no one would even miss me or care that I was not there. There was a time that I was even put out of a church by a Pastor after expressing that

I felt led to start a church. This of course was done after I had faithfully served under him for some time. I was accused of attempting to do something underhandedly, like stealing church members and operating with no integrity. The blow to my sense of confidence in other Pastors was severe. There seemed to be no concern from those who benefited by all that I tried to reach when I was there. By the time I closed the second church and walked away from it all, I lost all hope. Basically I was completely depressed.

The truth of the matter is that God's infinite wisdom far surpasses anything we can perceive or think. Like a good father, He not only knows what is best for our lives, He also knows how to protect our lives from what can destroy us, even ourselves. Father really knows best. The question is: Does God have expectations of us? The answer is simple. Yes. Remember expectations are a product of any relationship and certainly God is no different. In all honesty, it is very difficult to deal with the knowledge that we have failed God in what He may have expected of us. If you have enjoyed a relationship and fellowship with Him it is especially hard. Sometimes the burden of that reality can feel overwhelming. I submit to you, that is why many stray away and struggle to find their way back. You may be reading this right now and feel as though you are in that very place. Perhaps you are feeling lonely and empty, as though the familiar comfort of God's presence is but a memory. I am here to let you know that as long as you have breath in your body you can find your place back in the safety and comfort of His arms and rediscover the peace that only comes from God's love.

When we make an appointment to go see our doctor it could be because it is time for our checkup or we feel that something is not right with our body. We look for a sense of assurance from our doctor that everything will be okay. Amazingly, all of the anxiety experienced before we met with him or her seems to somehow dissolve without a trace, once we get the few words of assurance from someone we deem as an expert in their field. Or, if we find that something is wrong that our doctor will possess the knowledge and skills to correct whatever the ailments we are facing. We hold them in high regard because of their education and experience in a field we are unfamiliar and uncomfortable with. When we look at individuals who seem to have a grasp on arenas in life that seem to span beyond our scope of understanding, comprehension or abilities, there is a tendency to see them in much more of a greater light than as an average person. This certainly rings true concerning Pastors, our spiritual doctors.

But what happens when the way we view our doctor is altered due to a sickness that somehow impacts them. When we are suddenly struck with the reality of their humanity. Does somehow the way we interface with them change because of this discovery? We see this happen over and over again these days when people who we regard as great figures somehow are exposed due to an impending flaw in their life or character. What I have found interesting is that depending on our view of a person we will measure and administer our level of tolerance and/or forgiveness. For example, if the President of the United States makes a mistake, depending on the view of those who support and either voted him into office or those who opposed him, he will either be excused and forgiven quickly or he will be resented more and repulsed. We handle situations typically as we feel it is beneficial to us. It is much easier to sit as judge when it involves other people that are particularly in what we deem as elevated positions.

I opened this chapter with a scripture that highlights Jesus in the same type of critical light that all leaders face. During the public ministry of Jesus Christ there were literally thousands that benefited from his message and acts of miracles, love, and intervention. He was embraced as much as he was hated. No matter what your take may be on who Jesus Christ really was, secular and Biblical history agree upon his existence and the fact that he made a significant impact on the lives of so many people that still rings true today. Along the way, his greatest criticism actually came from those who should have been his greatest supporters, religious folks.

But what I would like to focus on is the people who sat and listened to Jesus' teachings and those who feasted on the food that miraculously was expanded to fill the stomachs of those who heard him teach on the hillside. Or even those whose homes he visited and performed divine healings. There were countless acts performed that were never recorded in the Bible. When things were at the height of Jesus' ministry everyone benefited by the things he accomplished. But at the moment of his most critical hour was when he revealed his greatest vulnerability to everyone. It was at that moment everyone's true faith in him or their disdain for him became most evident. At that moment, when he was being judged and condemned by the court of public opinion, that many who once enjoyed him now called for his death. At that defining moment it was not popular to sit at his feet and enjoy the enlightening words from his lips, but rather to take the side of the executioner. My point is that Jesus Christ did nothing to warrant such hatred, but even in his most gallant efforts there were those who rejected the notion of him being considered their savior because their depiction of him was less than what they felt someone who should be a king or messiah should look like.

In their minds Jesus was flawed because he did not rise to the level of expectancy that they carried in their minds. His neighborhood upbringing was an issue. Where he was born was an issue. Who his parents were was an issue. Even how he dealt with his opposition was an issue. So when the proverbial rubber met the road many of the people who profited by His efforts leaned on the side of popularity rather than stand firmly upon what they so conveniently benefited from months or years before. The physician from Nazareth who was responsible for healing so many others now was in need himself. He was repulsive to people who felt he should have personified perfection and flawlessness. He was beaten within an inch of his life and then crucified. It is not until it is all over that the recognition that he deserved is realized. It took years for history to depict the true essence of who He was. Here was a man who had no apparent flaws except in the minds of his skeptics, but he was treated less than how he deserved to be treated.

If the one so many called Lord and Savior was subjected to such heinous scrutiny and condemnation by mankind, where do those who serve in leadership who carry mantels of responsibility stand? Everyone who desires to function in leadership in any capacity should consider the cost of that obligation before committing to it. When I began my role as a minister I was under great disillusionment of what this undertaking would mean. I had no idea that my life would literally become such an open book to those who sat and listened to what I had to say. What was even more critical was the internal battles and conflicts that I faced and no one else really knew about. Whether I liked it or not my actions inevitably affected those who were a part of my following. I did not want it to be that way, but that is the cost of leadership. No matter how much we may want our actions and lives to be separate from the people who follow us, there is always a level of exposure that we are held accountable for. I always said I would never want to be a celebrity because I would not want that kind of exposure where everything I did was literally held under the microscope of public media and public scrutiny.

But even as a Pastor there was still some degree of exposure that I had to embrace. When I fell I often wondered just how many other Pastors were in a similar situation to where I now found myself. As a Pastor you are in the unique position of being a spiritual physician. While you may not practice internal medicine you do practice spiritual medicine. As Jesus put it so aptly, *"Those who are well do not need a physician but those who are sick"* (Matthew 9:12NKJV). So then that responsibility was passed on to those who were called to serve as His shepherds. But certainly the problem arises when those whom he has called to the responsibility of being a spiritual physician find themselves as sick as those they may be trying to heal.

Contradiction and hypocrisy are synonymous and can often be used or viewed in relevant terms as it relates to disappointments by those in leadership. Particularly when those who function in a leadership capacity are in a morally esteemed position. The person's failure to live up to the standard they represent can become an overwhelming let down. But I submit to you that the person in that position can also be disillusioned by what they perceive is right. In other words attempting to justify the wrong in their life instead of confronting and correcting the wrong. Long before the failure in a church or a relationship or a political office becomes public it is always being internally wrestled with by those who commit such wrongs. By the time it is brought to light by an array of media or personal gossip, the person or persons involved in the failure have already become either fully engulfed by their guilt or they have certainly numbed their guilt by justifying their wrong. The latter is the most dangerous. It is one thing to confront and wrestle with the wrong you may have been committing, it is another to attempt to excuse it. I think we have all been guilty at some point in our lives of attempting to justify something we may have done that was not right. The hard truth is what we continue to wrestle with in our society, that is wrong, and our efforts to try and excuse those wrongs.

When the news of the infamous scandal broke regarding the much esteemed Tiger Woods and his plight of infidelity in his marriage it was all anyone could do to not form an opinion of him as famous golfer and sports figure. There were so many sides to the opinions that came to the fore front of the media. The conversations were rampant everywhere, from the work place lunch rooms to sports bars and parking lots around the world. This man's life was in full view of literally the world and there was no place for him to hide his shame. Though he broke no secular laws of the land he was guilty in the court of public opinion. He violated his vows and shattered the trust of not only his wife, but also many others who looked up to him as an inspiration of excellence and accomplishments. Sponsors quickly distanced themselves and recanted promotional opportunities from him and other friends gave him a wide berth as not to appear as one who condoned his actions. The media coverage was never lacking in any capacity for what he did. His life was an open book and his flaw was evident to everyone who knew about it.

What I often wondered is out of everyone who was readily available to attempt to condemn his career and life to almost certain death, how many of them had similar flaws in their lives that had not been exposed? How many wrestled with the same addictions and immoral behaviors that Tiger did? It often seems like every day we are hearing about another type of scandal of someone in a visible role that is being put on public display for all to judge. It is not to suggest that any of the unfortunate failures we hear about are excusable actions. The direction that I am heading in is to show that while examining the obvious we must be mindful that the flaws that can plague another could easily be our own. This amazes me about human behavior.

I once attended a conference that was filled with people of various church backgrounds that featured guests and renown speakers and singers from a vast circle of denominational and non-denominational church backgrounds. What I found to be more entertaining than the conspicuous guests, who were on stage, was the vast audience that participated in the event. It amazed me how the perception of the people that stood in long lines waiting to get in would socialize and occupy the time by proudly boasting on their churches and Pastors and how great they were. I certainly applauded their seemingly unwavering support of their local shepherds. What I found more interesting was how many conversations I would hear of individuals prophetically speaking to selected people that waited outside, of how that person would one day Pastor a church. By the time we entered the building for the start of the evening's meeting there were at least twenty-five new churches formed by newly appointed Pastors who were called right there in line. As amusing as that may sound what concerned me as I walked away from that experience was how little understanding most of the people who shared in that exchange really had about what the role of a Pastor was about. Pastoring is so much more than what most people may see. Sometimes I wonder if many Pastors truly grasp the significance and impact of the role they fill. What I have learned is that our society carries varying expectation levels.

I was surprisingly amazed to learn that when it comes to our expectations of people, I have learned that populaces are typically categorized and viewed based on our mode of thinking. What can present great challenge to us is when our expectations fall because of the shortcomings of someone we have respected in their particular office, especially when we are directly impacted by their actions. The difficulty here is that our expectations often fall victim to humanity, after all we are human. I often grappled with the notion that somehow when I was in a position of responsibility such as a Pastor that I was to be everything that the role outlined me to be without exception. The problem was that I was still very much a work in progress. I struggled often with my imperfections and compared them with my Sunday performance on stage. The size of the congregation was completely irrelevant, it was simply the principle of not being what I preached that was the case of so many, ultimately being hurt by my own flaws. The irony was that the message that I taught was that God was a healer. I invited many to come to the altar and offered a prayer for whatever ailed them. "Trust in the Lord" was what I often suggested. Yet in all the sincerity that I was presenting there was the need for one more to come to the altar, "Me". I probably needed it just as much, if not more than many who did come. Please make no mistake, Pastors are not perfect by any stretch of the imagination, but they are expected to live by a standard that would simply cause them to find accountability a worthy measuring device. One thing, evident and certain is simply that in a capacity of leadership such as a Pastor or an Executive or Vice President of a corporation or a President of a group, there is a degree of transparency that is always associated with that role. With the transparency comes a level of expectation that while not always fairly assessed, often exists.

Healing the Doctor

I believe one of the worst things a physician can do is attempt to treat himself/herself when inflicted with a serious disease. While they may be an expert in their field, the same thing that they practice daily must be exercised by their own actions. Utilizing the skills and expertise of another physician to properly assess the condition of another physician is critical to their continued profession and personal health. While a doctor could assess certain things about himself/herself, there is no thorough assessment and treatment given without the assistance of another physician who is trained to address the same conditions they are trained to evaluate daily. Basically, physicians are not an island to themselves because there are multiple levels of accountability that are exercised by the higher authorities that license the physicians to practice their work. Liability risk is too great to take chances on rogue physicians who do not adhere to guidelines and stipulations that are part of the demand of their office. If a doctor finds himself/herself in a condition that compromises the integrity of their work they are encouraged to step away from practicing medicine until those areas are addressed and resolved properly. As the general public, we expect that what we experience with our physician is nothing but the best and that the organizations that back them represent our best interests. Our peace of mind is satisfied when we feel that the doctor has met all the criteria necessary to function properly and is in the best of health. While we realize that they are just as human as we are, we do expect there to be an elevated measure of standard that gives care to our concerns and assurances.

One of the things I have found myself concerned about as I looked at my own setbacks and failures as a Pastor was the type of pieces that were in place to aid people in my position. It stood to reason in my mind that if I struggled for years with issues of pornography and infidelity how many other Pastors were wrestling with the same issues. How many Pastors are struggling with alcohol and drug addiction? How many wrestle with issues of anger and verbal/physical abuse? How many are guilty of child molestation? How many have stolen from the ministries they serve? How many churches are led by sick spiritual physicians? After all, I was spiritual physician who was practicing in the office of a Pastor, but was in desperate need of treatment myself. It was never a question of competence or ability to teach or preach. It was not a matter of being able to articulate, it was a matter of accountability and spiritual health. I think sometimes the church, if not careful, can become consumed in church membership growth, media opportunities, ministry success and Pastoral popularity that it loses scope of the things that undermine the integrity of the calling.

In essence, the church is only as healthy as the Pastor. Until those areas are addressed, the church suffers a major deficit. Today, as church scandals seem to be common place in the media and the church community, I believe what we are seeing has become a pandemic of viral activity that has met many Pastors and churches with devastating results.

Whether the churches are smaller ministries or mega churches, the issues are universal and relentless to affect all aspects of the body of

Christ. The attempt is quite simple, to paralyze the efforts of the church from reaching those in need of salvation and hope. Pastors are clearly being targeted in unprecedented ways. Unfortunately there has not been enough done to address and work with Pastors who may be dealing with internal challenges. I remember wanting so badly to address the issues I dealt with but felt so embarrassed and isolated in what I was dealing with. While I can clearly admit that I was challenged with accountability necessities, I will also say that much of my contest had to do with the fact that resources and support were never readily in my reach. I found it to be so difficult to address the problems because there was never an advertised arena to deal with the apparent pitfalls of those in the Pastorate.

For me, it took a phone call to a very large church in Tampa in shear desperation that allowed me to finally get the help I needed in order to begin the healing process. My phone call was a last attempt effort to find aide and support to get me turned on the right path. I don't know if I sounded like a desperate man at the end of his rope, but I am so grateful that the Bishop thought enough to return my call. His willingness to call me gave me something I lacked, hope. For the first time in years, I felt a sense of hope concerning the deeply embedded issues that contaminated every good thing in my life. He agreed to send and pay for my healing process that would address every deep seeded issue that sprung up over the years. It was the best thing that could have ever happened to me. He sent me to Dallas, Texas for what would amount to a few weeks of intensive counseling that unearthed the hidden poison that killed all that was good in my life. To this day I am eternally grateful to Bishop Randy White, who did not know me from a can of paint, for stretching out his hand and helping me.

As I returned a much healthier man, I began to wonder how many more Pastors and Bishops and Apostles were in my regrettable position. This brings me to a point that I believe bares further scrutiny and examination. The concerns and challenges I present are in the arena of true accountability and support for those who function in such high and esteemed positions. Fortunately (or unfortunately) for me, I was part of a smaller ministry so the devastation was not as wide spread as one who may Pastor a mega church. When a Pastor from a church of that magnitude falls, the impact is far more reaching than what I dealt with. But it poses a question of what is that Pastor's circle of accountability and support. After all, the Pastor doesn't just suddenly fall. It is always a process which means it is an embedded issue that requires attention that is often neglected. But, if it means that it would require the Pastor to step down or take a sabbatical until there has been time to address and heal the issues, then what is the immediate impact? What is the long term impact? What is the financial impact? I submit to you that this brings up other more significant issues.

Many Pastors bolster at the notion of seeing what they have diligently worked hard to grow, flourish. Because of the ministry's success, many Pastors struggle and balk at the concept of changing their status to address a problem that could potentially derail their efforts and change the path of the ministry they serve. So as a result, much of what lies beneath the surface as a reality often goes left unchecked and consequently weakens the ministry and causes significant damage amongst the people they are called to serve. If true for smaller churches, can you imagine the impact of larger ministries and churches? When renown television Evangelist Jimmie Swaggart confessed to his infidelity in 1988 and Evangelist Jim Bakker in 1987 admitting his affair and scandal, it was the first time that major church leaders were being displayed in a light that illuminated the flaws of their humanity and inconsistency within the church. Today it is alarming to consider the widespread fallout of church leaders of the Catholic churches and the Pastors and Bishops in the evangelical churches who have fallen suddenly, being exposed to reveal their dark secrets that have ultimately brought damage to their personal lives and the churches they lead.

My questions are: where was the avenue of accountability that should have been in place to address the issues before they matured into a destructive force? Was it recognized before it escalated into something that brought embarrassment to the church and/or the family? If it was, who knew about it and what did they do to address it? Additionally, what happens if the Pastor or Bishop has become such a spiritual icon in the Christian community and is found flawed? Who holds them accountable, truly accountable? Is the church in a place where it is prepared to change the course of its leadership in the interest of righteousness or is there a greater yield and fear of revenue loss?

One thing that is a reality of the Christian community today in both the preaching and teaching vein, as well as Christian music arena, is that it has grown and developed into a multibillion dollar industry. Jesus once stated in Matthew 21:13, "*It is written, My house shall be called a house of prayer, but you have made it a den of thieves"*. I have often wondered how far has the church come from the concern that Jesus brought up with this issue so many years ago. How would He view what much of the church has become today when it comes to how we market ministry? I am not suggesting that this rings true for all churches; however, what I am saying is it would be irresponsible for there not to be an evaluation of how we present the gospel and the extent we will go to ensure its profitability. Are we so enamored by the desire to see our Pastors' and ministries successes that we would close our eyes to the truth of their condition? Has it become more important to see him/her travel in a corporate jet to minister the gospel in several of his/her churches than to ensure that he/she is a true reflection of the message he/she presents?

I feel that we do a greater disservice to the integrity of the gospel if we do not ensure that those who carry the mantel of delivery are in the best shape possible to present it. Please make no mistake, there are no perfect Pastors and every one of them has something in them that wreaks of imperfection, but when that issue becomes cancerous, as to bring the ministries they serve to a place of compromise, it must be addressed with the greatest sense of urgency.

CHAPTER FOUR

THE LAW OF RESPECT

This poor man cried out, and the Lord heard him, and saved him out of all his troubles. The angel of the Lord encamps all around those who fear Him and delivers them. Oh, taste and see that the Lord is good; blessed is the man who trusts in Him. Oh, fear the Lord, you His saints. There is no want to those who fear Him. The young lions lack and suffer hunger; but those who seek the Lord shall not lack any good thing (Psalms 34:6-10 NKJV).

Much of my time of recovery and restoration has been spent reflecting in a way that helped me to understand my mistakes and the root causes of them. I believe you can only grow from your mistakes if you learn from them. History is best utilized if we learn from it. History is the greatest instructor that God has given to mankind. But the issue or question is, are you willing to be a student and listen to what it says? History was given to us to learn from, rather than to live in. You cannot fulfill your life's purpose by living in your past whether good or bad, it cannot elevate you if you choose to live in it rather than learn from it. Sometimes I have felt like I would give anything to rewind the clock and start over again. That type of thinking is more reflective of regret. Regret of some quality or pointless decisions I have made in my life. Regret by definition is a feeling of sadness, repentance, or disappointment over something that has happened or has been done.

Regret is one of the hardest things to live with. I would love nothing better than to live in a way that I would never have any regrets in life. As wonderful as that may sound it is not at all realistic. The question is, without regrets would we really grow? Regrets are a signal of making a mistake that has occurred. I don't know of anyone who relishes the idea of making mistakes. Mistakes are an essential ingredient to wisdom and growth. For example, there are certain ingredients when I make my cakes, I don't like to eat separately. I don't like eggs raw and can't eat the cake raw. I would never drink the oil that has to be put in the cake mix. But if I don't put it in I won't get the outcome that puts the smile on my face when the cake is completed. We have all made mistakes in our lives and on some level you and I have faced something that we regret. But rest assure, there are regrets that can be very beneficial to our life's purpose. If we learn from our mistakes a regret can become a resource of wisdom that helps guide us in future decision making.

I have often reflected upon my child-hood as a time of innocence and fun feeling, believing that it was the best time of my life. I believed that I would love nothing better than to go back to those years of seemingly pleas-ant memories with the knowledge that I pos-sess today and change the course of my life. I have often thought that it was better then, than it is today. If I could go back there I would have done better in school and went on to college so I could have gotten my degree and perhaps life would be easier. I thought if I could do it all over again, I would have never chosen the person I was married to, I would have cho-sen a different person and I would have been so much happier.

What I was really saying, was that I had a desire to escape the current consequences of my recent or long past choices. I wanted to exist in a place much different from my current circumstances when I felt the pressure of negative conditions. After all, who needs all this pain and the challenges I was facing. And as great of a plan as it would seem to be to go back in time and undo or redo my decisions with my current knowledge there is a greater picture that must be examined, The Law of Cause and Effect.

Every choice has an impact whether good or bad. Please understand that our desire to undo things of our past is nothing new and is not uncommon. Even God has had moments of regrets. Yes the omnipotent, omniscient God relates to our feelings as well.

"And the Lord was sorry that He had made man on the earth, and He was grieved in His heart". **(Genesis 6:6NKJV)** *"I greatly regret that I have set up Saul as king, for he has turned back from following Me"* **(I Samuel 15:11NKJV).**

It would seem almost impossible to conceive that God would knowingly move forward with a plan that would somehow end up with disastrous results. However, what we must understand is, God's thought processes far exceed our own. At the end of God's purpose is a greater good no matter what the challenge. And what He uses is the painful process of disappointment and setback to extract glory for Himself that cannot be matched by flawless living. In other words, the greater the tragedy, the greater the glory revealed when the setback or mistake is overcome. But His purpose is not solely for His glory only, but for your benefit as well. Success does not come without challenge nor triumph without pain. That is, the cost and what makes triumph so great is the ability to endure painful experiences and overcome them through perseverance. God's promise to us is that no matter what, you can overcome your failures in life. *"And we know that all things work together for good to those who love God, to those who are called according to His purpose"* (Romans 8:28NKJV). Wouldn't it have seemed easier for God to redeem man from the comfort of His throne without the sacrifice of His son? It would seem to me that He could have merely spoken a few words as He did in creating man and "poof" man would be recreated all over again. However there would have posed a problem with that formula of remedy. For one, it would not have allowed God to demonstrate his infinite wisdom in resolving problems and cleaning up issues that we often create. Secondly, it would not have maximized the glory He enjoys so much and more significantly, it would have violated a principle that we'll examine, The Law of Respect.

Recently, God began to take me back down the path of my life to examine the root causes of failure. Not in a condemning way, but rather like a wise teacher and loving father instructing me in the finer principles of life. It was a journey that helped me to understand the reasons of cause and effect. As He shared with me the following thoughts:

Life is governed through various principles and laws that must be respected. In life there are many things that you and I will not like. However, just because we don't like something does not give us the right to disrespect it. Everything in life hinges on the principle of respect. Our relationship with God is based on this principle. Our country is governed on this principle. The cooperation between nations is based on it. It is to be adhered to for the safety and protection of our citizenship. The laws that have been posted on our highways were placed there for the adherence and safety of those who travel down them. You may not like to drive 25 mph around a dangerous curve and it may feel like an inconvenience to you especially when you are in a hurry, but the moment you decide to exceed it because you don't like it, you run the risk of facing the consequences of your actions because you did not respect it. Now the consequences can be either a ticket by the local law enforcement agency or a more extreme deadly encounter. Traveling motorists put traffic signals in place to govern our streets and preserve lives. But how many times have people ran a red light because they didn't want the inconvenience of being held up another three minutes, only to kill someone else or themselves because they didn't respect the vessel put in place to shield death. Whenever a law that is implemented, whether the law of God, the law of the land or even the law of gravity it should be respected. The violation or disrespect of these laws because we don't respect them will eventually lead to a negative outcome.

Much of the Bible and the teachings of Jesus Christ are founded and based upon love. His statement when asked what the greatest commandment, was to "love God with all your heart, soul, and mind. And the second was like it, which was to love your neighbor as yourself". This is at the foundation of His teachings. In fact on one occasion he stated *"if you love me you will keep my commandments"* (John 14:15 NKJV).

There seems to be very little about in the Bible on respect. However, it is embedded in every aspect of the consequences of what has gone against what God wanted for His people. The word that can be properly reflective of respect is "fear". The Bible encourages us to "fear the Lord". This is why I included the verses at the top of this chapter.

"This poor man cried out, and the Lord heard him, and saved him out of all his troubles. The angel of the Lord encamps all around those who fear Him and delivers them. Oh, taste and see that Lord is good; blessed is the man who trusts in Him. Oh, fear the Lord, you His saints. There is no want to those who fear Him. The young lions lack and suffer hunger; but those who seek the Lord shall not lack any good thing" **(Psalms 34:6-10 NKJV).**

It is not the type of fear that immobilizes us from approaching God or the type of fear to intimidate you from seeking Him. Rather, it is a type of fear that causes you to respect God. The word fear as it relates to God in the Bible is more accurately translated as respect. It makes sense when you think about some of the reasons for the calamity that has fallen upon the people in the Bible who disobeyed what God instructed. *"The fear (respect) of the Lord is the beginning of knowledge; but fools despise wisdom and instructions"* (Proverbs 1:7). The fear of the Lord is mentioned countless times in the Bible. It is synonymous with respect. Not only does God desire to be respected but there are great benefits associated with that type of reverence. *"Do not be wise in your own eyes;*

fear (respect) the Lord and depart from evil. It will be health to your flesh and strength to your bones" (Proverbs 3:7-8 NKJV).

Adam and Eve were dismissed from the Garden of Eden not because of merely eating the forbidden fruit. It was the lack of respect for what God instructed them not to do. Consequences followed their actions, which we still live with today. While many argue over what type of fruit Adam and Eve ate they missed the greater principle, respect. Once the laws of God were introduced, consequences were always associated if they were not respected. Disobedience of a command is a form of disrespect. When you and I refuse to obey something we essentially do not respect the directive or the person that has given the directive. This is what I believe triggers anger or consequences from the ones who initiate the directives whether good or bad. It is the reaction to a lack of respect. Everyone wants to feel respected. It is a natural part of our DNA to want to feel that moment of acknowledgement. It can literally help build a relationship and the lack of respect can certainly tear a relationship apart. To disagree with someone is one thing, but to disrespect someone is another thing. It takes the issue to an entirely different level and in many cases can cause irreparable damage. When we don't extend

one of the basic necessities of human existence which is to feel respected, we sow the
seeds of contention.

It is certainly just my opinion, but I really
believe that contention has been the root
cause for many of the social breakdowns that
we have seen in this country and countless
countries around the world. Much of what
fuels racial tensions in our country are rooted in
a lack of respect towards another race. Social
statuses may differ in every community and
culture; however, all men and women want
to feel that they are respected. Does respect
have to be earned? Certainly, but it is unjust
to expect to have the respect of those you
refuse to offer respect towards. In other words
respect must be mutually shared for the results
of elevated relations to be realized. If everyone really respected each other think of how
different our world, our country, our govern-
ment, our communities, and our families would
be. Respect does not remove disagreements
it merely redirects how we disagree. If I disagree with someone I respect, I will give him
or her, a much better feeling of confidence
towards our relationship and a better sense of
assurance of the outcome of the situation. But
if I don't respect the person I am having a disagreement with, not only is the disagreement
bleak, but also the relationship has been driven

further into the ground because of the disregard of how I view that person. So our perception plays a big part of how we respect. Many people will offer respect to people they feel they can benefit knowing.

CAN YOU SEE ME?

Have you ever approached someone that you admired, but never knew and attempted to engage in conversation with them only to be shrugged off like you were a fly hovering over their meal? How did it leave you feeling? Years ago I attended a church conference in Tulsa, Oklahoma where there were thousands of attendants who came for spiritual inspiration in the form of preaching and singing from some of the more renown gifted personalities within the church circle. Since Tulsa wasn't a huge city, after one of the evening sessions ended, everyone made his or her way to the local restaurants in search of a meal to enjoy before heading in for the evening. When we arrived at a particular restaurant I saw a gospel artist that I had admired for years. Being surprised by his presence at the crowded restaurant I felt that I wanted to merely tell him how much I enjoyed his music and how encouraging it was. Since he was standing in the lobby of the restaurant I thought it was not intrusive because he wasn't eating a meal nor engaged in a conversation. My comments were only going to be very brief and to the point. When I spoke with him he never gave me any sort of eye contact, but rather talked to me as though I wasn't even standing there. He literally talked over my head as if I were nothing more than an obstacle preventing him from getting to his final destination. What bothered me was not that he was obviously not interested in anything I had to say, but rather the lack of respect to even acknowledge my presence. Needless to say, it altered significantly how I viewed him and challenged my ability to receive his musical message again. For no other reason than feeling disrespected it took years for me to find the ability to look passed my experience with him personally and enjoy his music again. To this day my perception of him is still negatively altered.

Several years before that experience, I was on a flight with my mother traveling from New Jersey, on our way home back to Los Angeles. I was pleasantly surprised to find someone famous on our flight. Carol Burnett sat not far from the row where we were located. Again, I felt compelled to speak and say hello. I was very reluctant because I had no idea how she would respond. After all she was one of the most popular comedians and actresses of the time. My mother begged me not to go over there, but encouraged me to leave her alone. But I just wanted to say hello and tell her how much I enjoyed her as a child growing up. Surprisingly, she was one of the warmest and most engaging personalities I have ever met. We ended up having a great conversation that lasted for quite some time. I got more than I ever expected from her simply by her acknowledging my presence and receiving a simple compliment. That experience happened over 20 years ago and I have never forgotten how wonderful and gracious she was. To this day when ever my mother or I speak to people about that experience we both glisten with excitement. Not because she gave us anything special, but the most valuable thing you can give another human being is respect.

In both situations, one caused a negative response that forever altered my ability to receive anything this person put out. The other made me an even bigger fan. Whenever we become dismissive towards people who merely want the simplest act from us, which is respect, we can alter how that person views or interacts with us. However, if we offer the one thing that most people need even if it may not give them what they want we actually can gain their respect just by offering ours. Many people will only give you their respect if there is something that will benefit them. The artist that I was attempting to hold a brief conversation with would have probably been more engaging had I been someone he felt was beneficial to him.

The statement "familiarity breeds contempt" is certainly an accurate statement. What we become too familiar with in life can often serve to undermine our integrity. When something or someone we perceive as great in our life is new and unfamiliar, it will often arrest our respect because of the uncertainty of its or their potential. A new car, a new job, or even a new relationship, all command our respect. We take care of the new car like it's the last one on earth. We show up to work on time because we feel very blessed and privileged just to have a job. We treat the person new in our life like they were the greatest gift to ever enter our life. We respect them, all of them. This is due to the unfamiliar aspect of our understanding. Typically as we become more familiar, our tendency is to not hold it or them in the same regard that we once did. This is where our lack of respect begins to grow.

When someone takes drugs for the first time it doesn't take much to get them to a feeling of euphoria that they have never experienced before. Each time after that, more of the drug is taken to attempt to match the intense feeling they got the first time. So as a result more is taken each time to futilely equal the first experience. This is how addiction of any type becomes fueled. The more we remember the first experience the harder we attempt to achieve its match. Until we compromise all moral integrity and destroy everything good in our life in a failed attempt to reach our goal.

BROKEN RESPECT

So how does respect breakdown? Respect is the highest regard for what we behold. It is the foundation for what is built in relationships and serves as the fundamental practice for democracy. The question often posed; "Is it better to be feared or respected?" Indeed it is a question that most would answer, respected. I believe everyone wants to be respected. But what happens when we don't respect ourselves? Can we indeed respect others or God if we have no respect for ourselves? Self-respect is the key component to respecting other people and ultimately respecting God. Having no self-respect is a reflection of giving up on one's self. So then how does it break down in us and ultimately break down towards others? After all respect is learned behavior. It starts at home and branches into the streets, schools, and to people in general. If respect is not taught at home and there is no respect between parents and children then it typically will not be there for those outside of that home. Respect is a form of discipline, when you respect something you have a form of discipline towards what you respect.

Let's use the traffic signal as an example. We all get in a rush but there are times when I seem to catch every single light when I am in my biggest hurry to get somewhere. The lights seem to take an eternity to change and sometimes it seems like they purposely recalibrate the lights to take additional time to change before I get there. This of course does nothing but fuel the stress I am already feeling because I am behind schedule and/or am in such a rush to get where I am going. But no matter how much I am in a hurry to reach my destination, I must respect the law and the light because the consequence of not following such guidelines could be deadly. So I discipline myself to wait until the light changes before I proceed.

When we enter into a new relationship with someone, we often meet that relationship with our respect. We give them respect because we expect the same in return. We value how someone views us so we discipline ourselves in how we interact with them because we respect them. Whether we are physically in their presence or not we still offer our respect. This stays true to form until they do something that takes away our sense of respect towards them or something else breaks down within us. Somewhere that this is very evident is when we interview and start a new job. Because this is so important to us we give our potential or new employers the greatest form of respect. We show up dressed appropriately and on time (in most cases). In other words we discipline ourselves to give our greatest effort for the cause of the moment. What we feel is too valuable to not give our best effort, is what we give our highest regard.

When I joined the U.S. Air Force in 1984 the first thing that was drilled into our thought processes was discipline. It was and is the foundation for building a strong structure in life. They understood that if you don't have discipline you will have no success in what you are being trained to do. Discipline takes you from what you may or may not feel like doing, to a place of what you must do. Discipline is a reflection of self-control. It is indeed an outward reflection of an internal thought process. Self-control is a mindset, a resolve if you will. It is the reflection of a personal value system. It is the central point of where it all begins, is in the mind. Self-control is the central point that drives how we do various things in our lives, whether it is trying to manage how we eat or how we interface with people. It monitors what type of activities we allow ourselves to engage in. If you have no self-control you will have no discipline and if there is no discipline there is no respect. When self-control breaks down it is the result of fatigue that settles in, mental fatigue.

FEELING TIRED

Have you ever felt so tired mentally that things that were important began to fall by the wayside? I have often found myself in that position. Suddenly what I paid most attention to now seemed to lose its significance. My judgment became compromised and distorted when I began to feel mentally tired. When I look back at the valuable things I lost over the years of my life, much of it began due to fatigue. It took me years to realize the root cause of why it all began to slip away. Fatigue always sets in when we don't take time to rest ourselves or properly balance our lives. It is easy to stay caught up in the routines of our lives and daily habits. Many people get so caught up into everything they do, from day to day without exercising the benefit of balance. This includes those who work hard in the church circles. You can become such a diligent and

"faithful" worker and neglect the other important things in your life. Your perspective on
what you are doing will often fuel your judgment on the essentials of balancing. The hard
truth is that many hard workers from Pastors to
ushers often neglect the importance of their
own marriages and families for the responsibility of what the church calls, faithfully serving
the ministry. The Bible clearly calls for balance
and those who serve in the church should be
a reflection of healthy living outside the church
walls first. I Timothy 3:5-7 underscored the qual-
ifications of leadership within the church. Part
of the qualification is to be a healthy example
of balanced living both inside and outside the
church.

*"(For if a man does not know how to rule his
own house, how will he take care of the church
of God?); not a novice, lest being puffed up
with pride he fall into the same condemnation
as the devil. Moreover he must have a good
testimony among those who are outside lest
he fall into reproach and the snare of the
devil."(I Timothy 3:5-7NKJV).*

How does one rest the mind? Dr. Jack
Hayford a renown and respected Pastor and
author from California once wrote an article
that still serves as a reminder when I am beginning to feel peaked. He stated that our lives

are not unlike the gauges in the cars we drive. There are three gauges that are critical to our vehicles performance and survival. The gas gauge, the oil gauge, and the transmission gauge. All gauges are significant and critical to the engines survival and performance. They all require monitoring and must be respected equally. However, they all require various levels of attention. Your gas gauge runs out the quickest and it is what we pay most attention to when driving our vehicles. If our gauge breaks or we pay no attention to it, the results could be devastating. The oil gauge is something that requires less attention, but is equally important. If you don't monitor your oil and change it out routinely you could destroy your engine. The transmission gauge is one that is missed most often and yet requires just as much attention. To neglect the transmission gauge is to set yourself up for a costly repair bill that you may not be prepared to handle. So you have three gauges that require attention at different intervals.

We are built in a similar fashion. We have a physical gauge, an emotional gauge, a mental gauge and a spiritual gauge. All require attention but some can go longer without a change than other parts. When you are physically tired all that is needed is a good night's rest and your body is recharged and ready to carry on the next day's activities. It's a simple fix. However, when you become mentally tired you can go to sleep mentally drained and wake up with no change at all. Your mind is still in the same state as it was the day before. Because while we sleep our brains continue to function and consequently we remain mentally restless and needing resolve and repose from our state of mind. It often takes a change of venue or reprieve from the routine of our lives to recharge our mental condition. Or even more significantly, we often need a change of perspective. This often can come from hearing a very inspiring message from a Pastor at church or surrounding ourselves by someone that is positive and encouraging. Getting away and reading a good book or stopping to silence everything and everyone in our lives can also help us recharge our mental gauge. Sitting and praying and meditating are always good avenues to recharge our mental gauge. But what can be most helpful is to recharge our perspective on what we are doing.

How often do we sit back and consider what we are doing and why we are doing it? Is what you are doing in your life really benefiting you or is it draining precious time from your life? I believe that it is very important to consider what you think about and how you think about what you have in your life. When we get mentally tired we allow compromise to enter. If you have children you can get so mentally tired that things you normally wouldn't allow them to do, you suddenly yield to their constant pleas. Consequently, the results can be disastrous to them or everyone around them. What I think is most important is to realize where the limitations of your mental gauge ranges. If you don't monitor where you are mentally you can run the risk of making catastrophic mistakes that could be destructive in the long run.

When I was twenty-something... I worked as a Financial Aid Director at a business college. I had two very small children and worked very hard at the church I attended which was literally within walking distance from my home. I was working 12 to 14 hours a day at the college and coming home to an often challenging environment. I also was responsible for opening the church up every Tuesday and Thursday morning at 6:00 a.m. for prayer. Additionally, I drove the church van and served as a minister on Sundays and was expected to attend Bible studies on Wednesday nights. I spent so much time doing for everyone else, between my family, my church and my job that I neglected myself. I couldn't remember the last time I did anything for myself. If nothing else I took pride in being told that I was "faithful" to the church. It all came to a head one day as I woke up feeling what seemed like hair brushing against my forehead. As I kept trying to brush away something that was not there I arrived at work that morning and was told by an associate that I needed to look at the line of bumps that had formed on my forehead and go to the doctor immediately. After being seen I was told by the doctor that I contracted shingles. At that time I had no clue what shingles were and what they meant. Shingles is a virus that is typically thought to be brought on by stress. The doctor informed me that I should consider myself blessed that they did not form on the side of my head across my temple because if they had it could have easily killed me. I was instructed that I needed to take off work for the next 3 to 4 weeks. I was in no pain at the moment, but the doctor informed me that I certainly would be.

For the next two weeks, I experienced pain that I hope to never feel again as blisters formed on my forehead and down to one eyelid closing it shut. Today I still carry scars on that side of my forehead that serve as a reminder to me. But it wasn't until I went back to church for the first time after the sickness that an elderly woman took me outside in the parking lot to scold me and admonish me to never put myself in that position again, but always balance my life and take time for me. However, what I did not realize was how it also affected not only my body but my mental state as well. I suddenly found that what I once stood upon, never compromising my faith and values, suddenly took a turn for the worse. It became the gateway to compromise and ultimately a violation of my marriage. There are no excuses for infidelity, but what is important is that you read the signs of your mental gauge at all times. Take time to mentally recharge yourself. This won't happen overnight and you can't recharge yourself mentally if you don't take time to back away and decompress mentally. Remember, mental fatigue is what compromises our self-discipline and ultimately our since of self-respect and respect towards other people and things in our life.

Emotional gauges run the longest and consequently can often take the longest to recharge. When you become emotionally drained it is literally a build-up of something that has taken its toll on you, something that has reached its peak. For many people being emotionally drained can cause them to lose their will to survive. Impatience settles in and suddenly your will to function with integrity can become compromised. Emotional fatigue can be the most costly form of depletion. It is not something that will hit you overnight or will simply be based on a single incident. It is a result of days, months, and usually years of build-up. A marriage or relationship that has not been healthy, but rather abusive, volatile, and non-supportive can often lead to feelings of emotional fatigue. Your job can be the source of emotional fatigue. Surprisingly, it can and does often settle in the pulpit at church. Pastors can often become some of the biggest victims of emotional fatigue. The call of service and the balance of life can often conflict when there is not a proper perspective given to the Pastor. I often wonder why there aren't more opportunities presented to support these men and women who are never short of dealing with countless problems. When I look back over all the years I served in ministry for what often seemed like thankless efforts given, I did not take the time necessary to properly rest my emotional state of mind and I certainly did not weigh the importance of monitoring my emotional and mental gauges. Many Pastors can and do serve their congregations faithfully for years without properly balancing their efforts and ultimately their families and memberships will suffer for this.

The pressures of growing a church and reaching people become the greatest push of Pastors. When I examined the fall-out from my years of service I realized that I really operated on very little emotional strength. Was it enough to understand the Bible? Was it enough to understand church doctrine and budgets? Was it enough to understand community demographics and the impact of the local church? Apparently it wasn't. I understood all of those factors and yet at the end of the day the results were disastrous. I had not dealt with my fatigue factors, so how could I possibly have expected a victorious outcome. The emotional fatigue can and often does lead to the compromise of moral behavior that creates the destruction of relationships, churches, families, and communities. While I am pointing out Pastors, I need to emphasize that the same principle applies to anyone in any given situation. No matter what your field of work may be or what you may do there must always be a balance in your life and you must monitor your gauges.

When I am mentally tired I like to retreat to play golf or basketball and sometimes simulated flying and it often does the trick for me. Sometimes just a drive in my car with either relaxing music or no noise at all helps me to settle. Other times just getting away for a moment to put myself in a peaceful environment can be the soothing experience that helps me to relax. For you it might be a nice soothing bath or massage that helps ease the tensions of the day and help recharge your mental state of mind. Perhaps getting with friends and just doing something you really enjoy doing that has nothing to do with what you do on a daily basis is healthy and can be invaluable. But when you are emotionally drained, none of what I have stated will recharge your battery. Our emotions are a part of what makes up our souls (our soul is made up our mind, will, intellect and emotions); so therefore, what impacts our emotions impacts our souls. So it is critically important that we monitor what we allow to impact our emotions. This is why relationships are so critical to our emotional base and state of mind. When God desires to massage our emotions, He always addresses what is unhealthy so as to produce greater emotional strength within us.

Then there is a matter of our spiritual gauge. No matter what your religious affiliation, whether you consider yourself Baptist, Methodist, Apostolic, Lutheran, Non-Denominational or Catholic you have a spiritual gauge. This gauge is based upon your connection with God directly and reflects your time and connection with Him. The less time you spend with Him the less spiritual strength you will operate with. Spending time means the time you devote to studying the word of God and to praying. Like any relationship, if you want more from it you must put more into it. None of the other things I mentioned to charge the other gauges will work in the spiritual gauge. There is only one solution to resolve an empty spiritual gauge and that is spending time with God. When was the last time you just sat and spent time alone with Him studying the Bible? Fortunately, it doesn't take a monument of time to feel your meter replenished. Just taking some time to shut down the other areas of your life to give God some qualified, quality and uninterrupted time can satisfy the need. You should take a moment and turn off the TV, DVD, CD, DVR, VCR, iPhone, iPad, iTunes, laptop, desktop and just walk into a moment of complete silence and prayer. You would be amazed when you really tune into God, what things He has to share with you that would give you the strength and answers you have been looking for.

It's not that God doesn't want to address your concerns, but it is so easy to become distracted by all of the things that demand your time daily. If you have had a thought that you need to spend more time reading the Bible or praying then, there is a reason that thought came to you. Your meter is low. Don't depend on just mere church attendance to do the job. That is like eating once a week. It isn't enough to strengthen you to make it through the whole week. Many people look to pour their feelings and concerns out to God, especially when they are feeling overwhelmed with life's challenges. There is nothing wrong with expressing your thoughts with God. But the question is, do you take time after doing all the talking to sit in total silence and listen to His response? That is truly where the peace comes from. Once again, as in any relationship there should be a dialog in order to have a healthy exchange and not merely a monolog. The problem comes in when all we do is give God our monolog of concerns, but never take the time to hear what He has to say. So next time you pray before you get off your knees, take a moment to sit back, completely quiet and hear what His voice shares to illuminate your understanding.

So what do all four gauges look like? Simply put, it is like looking at an endurance meter. When our gauge is full physically, mentally, emotionally, and spiritually we are able to endure many things. As our gauges deplete, we are less able to handle things physically, mentally, emotionally, or spiritually the same as we would on a full tank. It's like playing a video game and your character begins to weaken as the strength meter fades after every blow of the opponent. Patience runs thin and what is seemingly important can deteriorate as we compromise the most important of things. What does a gauge look like when it is completely empty? In a word, compromise. We are either enduring when our gauges are completely full or we are compromising when they are completely empty. Our communities can either endure or compromise, depending on their make-up and the state of those who live in them. The stronger and thriving the families are, the stronger and more thriving the communities will be. The weaker and less thriving the families are, the weaker and less thriving the communities will be. Since our families, communities, and churches are made up of individuals, it is critical to keep your gauge as full as possible, in order to give your surroundings the greatest of strength you can offer.

RESPECT'S CONSEQUENCES

One of the hardest things I had to come to grips with once everything came to light in my situation was to look at what I would have to live with because of the destruction. God forgave me for everything I had done. I realized that many people struggle with coming to grips with God's forgiveness of sins. And for various reasons we may often feel that there is no way He could ever forgive some of the things we have done. But the truth is that He is very forgiving of the sins we commit in life. However, what He does not remove are the consequences we may face because of the choices we made.

God implemented the Law of Respect so like any other law, there are consequences to disobeying it. As I mentioned, when we choose not to respect people or institutions there can be dire consequences associated with those decisions. In my case because I did not respect the house of God or the people of God who attended the church I pastored, there were things I would have to face as a result of my choices. This would truly test the measure of my repentance and brokenness. I realized that in order to set things right before God I had to also set things right amongst the people affected by my actions.

I took a plane trip back to my home state of California (I lived in Florida at the time), unannounced I went to the people who I affected, including my children and ex-wife and asked each one of them to forgive me for what I had done. I felt like I owed them the respect of acknowledging their hurt and taking ownership of what had happened. I had no idea of what reactions I would get from anyone. I went to my Pastor and members of my church family and asked their forgiveness. Everyone I came to was caught off guard and very surprised at my actions. Every last one of them reached out and embraced me and told me that they forgave me. I realized also that some still held some hurt and resentment which I expected, but at the end of the day, all of them told me how much respect they gained for me because of my courage to apologize.

The most astonishing thing is that the Law of Respect brings about consequences both positive and negative. When you do something that causes others to feel disrespected, the results can be extremely devastating and painful. When you insult the person you are disrespecting, the results are reflective of wounds that can run very deep. The reactions you may face may be even more severe. However, when you do something that is viewed as honorable or respectful the results can be so much more rewarding, that you can't even put a monetary value on them. Regardless of how we may feel in life or about the choices we make every day, always seek to respect what you are confronted with and I assure you that you will go much further in life, rather than facing the negative consequences of disrespect. One of the areas that served to benefit me in recovering the respect that I so painfully lost was by exercising in the area of honesty. It is not surprising to know that when you walk down the alley of secrecy it can ultimately cause you to lose the respect of so many people, once the truth of your activities in the alley comes out into the streets. I found that people need the ability to make a decision on their view of you, based on truth and not what is perceived truth. To give someone the truth about who you are and be honest with them about what you feel or think, affords them the opportunity to form their thoughts based on factual truth instead of something that is not real. When I reached a place of "completely bottoming out" in my life, I had nothing left but the truth of who I was. There was nothing to cover up, but I could be honest with others about where I had been. Today, people can choose to embrace me or not embrace me, but what I have gained is respect from them all.

Let me point out what respect is not. Respect is not living your life everyday apologizing for everything you do or have done. It is important to confront and address the areas where you may have fallen short, but once that has been done you must continue to live your life in a way that assures a positive direction. One thing I certainly learned the hard way was that I could not expect to have a cohesive life filled with opportunity and peace without first addressing and confronting the mistakes of my past. That can be the most difficult part because of fear often associated with telling the truth. The fear of not knowing the reactions of those affected by your actions. The fear of the uncertainty of what you may face. All of these are factors that can sometimes make you reluctant to addressing your past situations.

However let me point out, by the same token that you can't advance in life if you are constantly made to look back to where you came from. You are sure to wreck yourself in that process. Make no mistake about it, there will always be an element of people who seek to hold you hostage to the past and mistakes you have made. It is imperative that you not allow yourself to be arrested by something you have already addressed in your life. Deal with it then move on from it.

I feel that many relationships are never truly mended because the honesty of what has challenged them has never been revealed. If you are looking for God to bless you in certain areas of your life it is a great way to open the gateway by being honest with people. At the end of the day people may not always like or agree with what you may have to say, but if you are honest, they will respect you for it. To deceive people is to build a false relationship because it is not based on truth. So the respect is not based upon truth. Consequently, when what we carry is exposed the first thing that is compromised is the respect that was once carried for us.

Once I embraced the Law of Respect, I found out that was all that was needed all along. The recovery started with just being honest with myself and what I had done and the rest was learning to find my way closer to God. This would prove to be challenging for me because it wasn't a question of whether or not God had forgiven me for everything that I had done, but rather me forgiving myself. The shame I carried was overwhelming, and at times too much for me to swallow, because, ultimately my greatest fear was, not being able to be used again by God. After all, everyone wants to feel like they are still usable and not used up.

CHAPTER FIVE

...AND PETER

"But go your way and tell His disciples and Peter that He goes before you into Galilee: there you will see Him as He said to you" (Mark 16:7NKJV).

One of the most difficult things I had to confront besides looking at the weaknesses and failures of my life was how to pick up and move forward. It was very difficult as I wrestled with the notion that my opportunities in life were fully exhausted. The eerie feeling of finality began to creep in and suddenly I felt the wind was leaving the sails of hope for my life. What felt strange was a question that would rise up that I could not seem to find the answer, which was simple, what do I do now? The only thing harder than falling, is trying to pick your-self back up as though you had never fallen.

I looked upon the scripture noted above that I actually taught on several years ago, but never thought I would find myself living it out. To gather a full appreciation of where I am going with this it would be a good idea to read about the story of Jesus' apprehension by the Roman soldiers in (Matthew 26:69-72).

When we look at the apprehension of Jesus Christ, one of the obvious targets of blame is Judas. We see Judas as the epitome of betrayal and he becomes the poster child of our expression of disappointment towards someone that has wronged us. His name is used as the punch line of jokes and is also the tool needed to bring our point home when we have experienced treason. He is synonymous with all we feel is the ultimate destruction of relationships. His betrayal is obvious and appalling to anyone who reads or hears the story of his selfish acts. Jesus himself acknowledged his plight by stating, *"It would have been good for that man if he had not been born"* (Matthew 26:24NKJV). But as much as it is apparent to us, there is another aspect that I would like for you to consider with me.

Peter, who is one of Jesus' closest disciples whom the Lord informed, would deny him three times before the cock crowed in the morning. This statement is made after Peter gallantly claims that he would never leave Christ. Peter's proclamation was made in the most confident yet arrogant manor. He was not only making his case to show Jesus how strong he was, he was also making a statement to the rest of the disciples. Peter's resolve was clear and his objective was obvious to all. Peter was filled with great ambition, but what he lacked was a sense of humility. His focus was not upon pleasing God, but rather pleasing himself and impressing the other disciples.

I used to look at the life of Peter and could see certain things about him that I found contemptible. I approached him in a judgmental capacity. But as I looked closer at him, I found much of myself in him. Peter was in ministry with Christ and he was also full of ambition and drive. But there were times when it became apparent that he was clearly trying to make a name for himself. He wanted to appear as one who knew everything there was to know about Jesus and take the forefront of representation.

When I entered ministry at 19 years old, as I look back on those days, it is clear that I wanted so much to be noticed in the ministry. I wanted people to recognize that I had a gift worthy of the audience of people in the church.

I wanted someone to acknowledge the fact that I had strengths that qualified me to speak before masses of congregates. The reality was that I was trying to compensate for the lack of personal achievement that rode my back, like a well fitted back pack. I wanted to feel like I overcame my past failures by somehow being elevated in church ministry and in the court of public opinion. I was just using my calling as an opportunity to express that resolve to the church and to anyone who would hear me. But amazingly, I was blinded to that fact that what I really felt was that I had to prove myself a success. Don't get me wrong, striving for success is not wrong, but the motive in which you strive must be driven by pure intentions. I was not in it just for the notoriety, but I did want to help people. My desire for helping others was clearly maligned with an ulterior motive, to also help myself.

When I was very young I had an ambition to become an airline pilot. I really did not connect with anyone and really had no mentor to steer me in a way that would help me accomplish this goal. So in high school I did not focus nor achieve anywhere close to my potential. As a matter of fact I hid myself in playing something that I felt I was halfway decent in, tennis. I played tennis all day every day and settled for poor grades and ditched many of the classes

I was supposed to take. I was acting completely contrary to what I wanted to accomplish. What I really wanted was to attend UCLA and graduate then get trained to become a pilot. When it was all said and done my class graduated without me and I was forced to look right into the face of failure. My next option was to join the U.S. Air Force. So a friend and I went to take the test to gain entrance. Unfortunately, because I had not focused on my studies in school, I did not pass the test initially. In fact, I actually got sick during the first test. Boy, nothing said failure to me than to not have graduated high school and not only fail the test to enter the service, but get sick in the process. I proceeded to try to circumvent the process by attending a city college, and still I did not finish those classes I signed up to take. This period began a process and habit that would follow me for several years to come. Starting something but not finishing it.

Have you ever found yourself guilty of that same pattern? I applied and got my GED since I had not graduated hoping that would somehow salvage my damaged ego and give me some semblance of accomplishment. When I met with my recruiter for the Air Force he informed me that a GED was unacceptable and that I would still need my diploma. In the meantime, I went and took the test again for the Air Force. Again I failed the test and found myself spinning downward in confidence. If I was to have any type of career in the Air Force I was going to have to face what I failed. I enrolled in adult education with a local high school to complete the classes necessary to gain my high school diploma. I felt so embarrassed because it was something I should have never had to resort to doing. But because I did not discipline myself in the prior years of high school, I was paying the price at that time. In the midst of the classes I was forced to take, I went for a third time to take the test to enter the Air Force and unfortunately for me, three times was not a charm. I failed again. Can you imagine how much humiliation I was feeling at that moment?

It was almost unbearable, as hopelessness and frustration began to oppress me. The cloak of shame began to creep in, slowly suffocating any glimmer of self-confidence that I possessed. I felt as though time was running out on me to accomplish my goals. I finally finished the classes I attended and was granted my high school diploma, which I needed to join the Air Force. I could not completely rejoice for that accomplishment because I still had not passed the test to enter the service. The interesting thing about that experience was that while my test scores were not high enough to go into the Air Force they were high enough to go into other branches of the military. The problem was that for me, there was no other option but the Air Force. So that meant only one thing. I had to pass the test no matter what. It wasn't until the eve of my fourth attempt that I did what I should have done the first time. I took the book that helped me to prepare for the test and I literally sat up all night in my parents' living room and prayed and studied. I rotated all night from the books to my knees determined to finally achieve my objective. So when the time came for me to take the test I finally passed. I had my diploma and the test scores necessary to enter the Air Force. The lesson I learned, looking back on that experience, was the importance of doing things the right way and taking all of our concerns to God for guidance and support.

Peter was a leader with a great call on his life taking on tremendous responsibilities. It is clear that he desired to do something great. If you look closely at Peter's actions as he followed Christ he was willing to do whatever was necessary to demonstrate his faith and his ambition. Peter was the only person to ever walk on water besides Jesus. He ultimately succumbed to his surroundings then sank but he walked first. Then at the most critical time Jesus reached down and pulled him up. How many other disciples can actually say they have walked on water? For that matter how many people can say they have walked on water? You may know people who act like they can or have walked on water, but how many people actually can say that is something they have accomplished?

We can celebrate Peter's zeal, but we must also look at his challenges. He didn't always get it right but his heart was in the right place. This was why he was chosen by Jesus to follow him in the first place. Peter was a man complete with ambition but often lacked humility. One of the great prerequisites of following God and truly becoming a great person that can be used by Him is choosing the road of humility. By the time we see Peter at the time of great persecution he folds like an envelope and withers into the background of shame and despair. Not once but three times he was confronted by a variety of people who pressed him regarding the nature of his association with Jesus. All three times he denied his involvement with Jesus. On one occasion he is filled with so much pressure and stress that he began to curse at the person questioning him.

Whenever you and I feel pressure and things are not materializing as we plan, we can often react in ways that are contrary to what we may believe. The true nature of what is in a person comes out whenever pressure is applied. Whether it is a matter of integrity and moral values, bad habits, bad language, or corruption. The true nature of what is in you will always come out as the pressures of life are applied. It is very easy to say what you and I would or would not do given a set of circumstances, but that is only a theory until we are actually put into that situation. If you want to test how strongly your values have taken root in your life, allow pressure to intensify and you will discover just how much is really there. Honestly, the thought of that has often frightened me. It means that I would have to look honestly at something that I may or may not want to see. Isn't it interesting how easy it is to examine and critique the lives of others, but sometimes very hard to deal with our own? The true essence of what we carry only comes out in the most critical of times. We either rise to the occasion or sink like a heavy rock. But whether you rise or sink there is always a lesson to be learned. Make the most of it.

SHAME ON YOU

Once Peter realized what he had done after hearing the cock crow and remembering what Jesus said to him about his failure, the fulfillment of that prophetic word came crashing down on him like a ton of bricks. He found himself overwhelmed with grief and sadness. The question is, was Peter's denial of Christ a form of betrayal? It is very easy to look at Judas' actions and serve him up on a platter. But to look upon Peter as a betrayer is another matter. Have you and I ever committed such abandonment towards God or others like this before, when someone really needed you and you knew they were counting on you and you bailed out on them? Or have you ever down played your faith in God to keep from being viewed as a fanatic or an unrealistic person? Perhaps something as simple as no longer giving God time in your personal prayer life or meditation, when you were once committed? Maybe like me, you once attended church because of your devotion and commitment to God, but now it only seemed like a commitment to people and an organization. Now you find yourself completely outside struggling to find your way back in.

Peter's guilt became stronger than his calling and suddenly Peter is found sobbing uncontrollably. His tears were laced with anguish and bitterness. He is clearly inconsolable. All of a sudden his ambitions and his calling were put into perspective. But what was conceivably at the base of his guilt was a sense of shame. Shame is so difficult to overcome that it can serve as an agent that keeps you under mental, emotional, physical and spiritual arrest and duress. Shame is directly associated with your past and it is something that must be conquered in order to move into your destiny. Shame is the cousin of guilt and it is there to constantly remind you of the guilt associated with your former actions.

When I confronted all of the failures of my past, I had no choice but to confront the shame as well. Shame ultimately will keep you from sharing your story of how you have overcome situations in your life. If you were a victim of a bad experience you must confront the shame associated with it in order to move forward. Shame can sit on you like a massive weight. If you choose to carry it, it will follow you wherever you go. You can pack your bags and move across the country and believe me, when you arrive at your destination it will be there to greet and welcome you to your new home. Certainly it is a tool that the enemy will use to stop any form of progression in your life. The reason shame is often so hard to overcome is because it attaches itself to your conscience. This is where you and I must exercise caution because what we never want to lose is our sense of conscience. When you numb your conscience to right and wrong, you position yourself to conduct any conceivable act without fear of consequences. Shame becomes the anchor that immobilizes you from any form of advancement. The question then becomes, can God use shame to benefit His will? In a word, yes. I believe God can use shame to remind us of how severe and destructive our choices have been. It essentially can be used to give us a moment of pause before moving forward to advance ourselves.

People can often become the symbol of shame in your life if you aren't careful. When you look upon people you have impacted in a negative way or have experienced something negatively from them, they can often serve to highlight the shame that looks to ensnare you. It took years for me to face people that my actions impacted. The shame was too overwhelming for me. Just the notion of seeing them or hearing something they had to say to me was so emotionally engulfing that I couldn't handle the thought of addressing them. Often women who are victims of rape experience this in tremendous ways. Young men who have been molested often face this tragic encounter. Shame knows no boundaries and is not discriminative towards any one gender or race or social and economic status. Shame's only objectives are to shut you down and shut you up. Shame's desire is to silence the voice that God has placed in you to help others live free from what may have sought to destroy their lives. In order to not be a slave to your past, you can't be a slave to shame. If you allow it, shame will rob you of opportunities to succeed in life and will hinder relationships you look to develop.

ALONE WITH SHAME

When I look back over my experiences, what I tried to do was live alone with shame. That was a horrible experience because I had no one who was in a healthy condition to be able to speak to my circumstances or my feelings. There was no one there to offer guidance nor support. Shame on the other hand, will be your best companion if you allow it to be. It is the one type of relationship you don't want to have. It will keep you company in the middle of the night and have you doing things you would have never conceived you would do. Shame will keep you disconnected from people who can offer you the best of support and help. I found shame to be relentless in its efforts to keep me from moving forward and getting over the past. Shame is the epitome of hopelessness. It always keeps you feeling helpless and hopeless. The ironic thing about shame is that if you allow yourself to be restricted by its grip, you will find that it will keep feeding you to any type of addiction you may have. It would suggest that you have no other alternative in life, but to do the only thing that may feel gratifying to your flesh. For some it may be drinking, others it could be drugs, and others sexual addiction or pornography. These are things that are all associated with shame.

It has been a proven fact that addictions are directly associated with shame. So whatever you may find yourself addicted to, please understand that shame lies at the base of your addiction. I believe the key is to understand what the shame is associated with in your life and not allow it to prevent or ground you from moving forward. It is hard to persevere when you are constantly facing continual setbacks because of shame. Granted, there are people who will do just as good a job at keeping you a prisoner of the past, as well, if you let them. If you aren't careful, shame will stand as the guard at your prison door and keep you from crossing the threshold of opportunity.

If you can imagine after Peter's denial of Jesus he was forced to now live with a decision that was made in a matter of seconds. Each denial of Jesus took Peter less than 10 seconds to accomplish, but the impact of those choices were felt for quite some time longer. There isn't much said in the Bible about Peter after his denial and weeping uncontrollably until we read about him in the book of Acts. This makes me believe that he was tucked away in hiding, left to deal with his shortcomings.

THE HARD PLACE

What a challenge it can be to pick up and dust yourself off and move forward with more confidence than you had before you fell. As I stated in Chapter two, I don't believe anyone can really do anything to us worse than what we do to ourselves mentally. What I found to be a great obstacle in my life was not merely confronting the impact of my mistakes, but also recovering from them. It took literally years for me to be able to walk back into a church and actually enjoy a service without experiencing the oppressive feelings of guilt and shame. When I would walk inside of a church service, I sometimes felt an over bearing sense of unworthiness. I did not want to be acknowledged in anyway. I wanted to sit in the back of the church in the deepest corner and blend in with the crowd, just melting away in the midst of the inspirational services. It has been said that to move forward into your future you must reconcile with your past. For years I struggled to not only find God's forgiveness for what I had done in the past but, to also find forgiveness, self-forgiveness. I did find that God's forgiveness was freely given to me, but it took many years for me to embrace that concept. Simply because I found that I could not forgive myself for some of the things I did, I could neither embrace God's love nor forgiveness. How on earth could God have forgiven me? What I found to be an interesting struggle was trying to come to grips with feeling disqualified for service and trying to get closer to God at the same time. I found myself in a paradigm shift.

"Two men went up to the temple to pray, one a Pharisee and the other a tax collector. The Pharisee stood and prayed thus with himself, God, I thank You that I am not like other men, extortioners, unjust, adulterers, or even as this tax collector. I fast twice a week; I give tithes of all that I possess. And the tax collector, standing afar off, would not so much as raise his eyes to heaven, but beat his breast, saying, God, be merciful to me a sinner! I tell you, this man went down to his house justified rather than the other; for everyone who exalts himself will be humbled, and he who humbles himself will be exalted" (Luke 18:10-14NKJV).

This is a parable of two men who go to the temple (church) to pray. One was a Pharisee (professional church authority) and the other a

Publican (tax collector). The Pharisee is a self-righteous faithful member of the church who comes to God in prayer and begins to belittle those who were not in church and even the tax collector who came to pray. His words are filled with arrogance and pride. There is no love for anyone, but himself, as he is very quick to point out others' shortcomings and sins. He feels his justification is in his commitment to doing all the "right" things that are required according to the laws of Moses and the traditions of church. He spends time fasting and in prayer. He pays his tithes and does all the things that often we find "acceptable" within the church. You don't have to look far to find him in the weekly services because he is there faithfully. He also is well versed with the things that are expected of him in the temple. He is religiously driven, but it is clear that he is not relationship driven. He seems to find his strength in his service to the temple and keeping the laws of God, but he lacks the ability to connect with those God desires to reach. Which begs the question: How do you truly connect with God without connecting with the people He desires to reach? Not only is the Pharisee out of touch with reaching others, his words are filled with disdain and condemnation.

The tax collector, on the other hand, is a man who has come into the temple out of sheer desperation. He has had to muster the courage to enter the temple in the first place. He enters humbled by his failures in life and lack of obedience and connection with God. He has realized that he does not qualify to be found worthy of his own accord so he embraces the throne of God with the arms of true humility. When he comes to God, he can't look Him in the face because of the array of shame that cloaks his being. He has found the definition of contrast not at the altar in the front of the church, but rather from the last row in the back of the church. He sees God's righteousness and his unrighteousness. He wears no mask nor does he try to disguise himself as being anything or anyone other than who he is. In the purest form, he shows God something that He clearly knows, but no one else is able to see. His heart, it is the one thing that God measures a man by, beyond anything else. He does not come in with a concern of someone else's faults or shortcomings, but only his own.

It is in this parable that we discover the true essence of what God looks for when we approach Him in prayer, church and service. Jesus applauds the Publican and shuns the Pharisee. He clearly is not moved by longevity or rehearsed church philosophy and traditions. Let me clarify, the things that are instituted in church are important and have their places, but they can't replace the importance of true humility and remembrance of the need of repentance by all. I once found myself very much and unintentionally as the Pharisee, but now I am transformed into the Publican. Once upon a time it was very easy for me to look at the faults of others with a sense of self-righteousness. I could easily run down to the front of the church and grace the pulpit in all my sense of arrogance and justification. Later, I struggled to find the courage to sit on the last row. I could not look up to God, let alone face those who served Him. There were so many Sundays that would come when I would awake and try and talk myself into getting up and going to church. I would soon after find a convenient reason not to go. It was so ironic that once upon a time you couldn't keep me from going to church now it was very easy for me to stay away. My shame kept me under such a tight grip that no matter how much I tried, it would reel me back in before I could decide what to wear. I would somehow try to convince myself that I was going to go the next week and would quickly bury my guilt by doing something else that kept me occupied. I couldn't even watch the local church ser-vices on TV without the feeling of shame and guilt. Weeks turned into months and months turned into years. I kept myself away from the house of God. I used every convenient excuse

I could think of including my inability to connect with a Pastor.

Amazingly, as much as I did things to keep myself away from the church, my heart longed to get back into the place I knew I was supposed to be. There were moments when I would seek to find ways to connect but couldn't find them. If there was nothing else more certain to me at that time, it was the reality that I was clearly lost. The lost sheep, I preached it and taught it for years, but I was now living it. What I had to come to grips with was the fact that I would never Pastor again. My interpretation of that harsh veracity was that it was epitomizing failure to me. I could not seem to grasp it and it was so very difficult to swallow. My thoughts were that God was finished with me completely.

Where do I go from here?

What I learned in the process of resolve was that God can't and will not fail. They used to sing in church that "there is no failure in God". It often felt like a cliché in the biggest sense until I went through my experiences. What I had to realize was that to understand if God were finished with me completely, I would not even be writing this book. I would be nothing but a memory in the minds of those who knew and loved me. Ministry for me was not ending, it was changing and I had to learn to embrace the change that God was making in me for the benefit of those around me. Perhaps as you read this you might find yourself at a similar fork in the road, conceivably feeling as though time has passed you by and you are wondering what God has in store for you now.

When Peter found himself in the position of shame and humiliation, what was needed was clarity of what God would do with his apparent failure and embarrassment. The beauty of what the scripture (Mark 16:7) depicts is God's earnest desire to remind Peter that he was not forgotten despite his failure. This is why his name is singled out in the scripture. Peter clearly removed himself from the rest of the disciples and God was now calling him back. There was a greater purpose that Peter had to now embrace. There is no greater feeling after you have failed in some form or fashion than finding that God still loves you and has more for you to accomplish. Everyone wants to feel useful and have a sense of purpose to keep themselves motivated. Can you imagine Peter's reaction when Mary Magdalene and Mary the mother of James and Salome, came and told him everything the angel just shared with them? Their words lifted the weight of shame that he was carrying. It sparked new life into him and suddenly he was walking again with purpose and confidence in God. It is simply amazing how much of a difference God's words can make in your life just by acknowledging your existence through someone else.

Recently, a Pastor I served under for a number of years came to Los Angeles to attend classes for a doctorate program he was taking. His stay was only for two weeks and in the time he was here we got together a couple of times to have dinner and hang out. It was a very gratifying and sometimes an emotional experience because of the realization of what we have gone through as friends and the fact that we came out of it as friends. What stirred my soul deeper than anything else that was said to me was a comment he made the last day of our visit.

I have sat back like the Publican in the parable we looked at earlier and watched how God has blessed my friend's church to grow. When I joined his church in 1991 there weren't more than 125 people in attendance. I served as his personal aide and ultimately became his Assistant Pastor until I left to start my own church. Today the church is well into the thousands in membership with multiple church services. There are dignitaries who proudly call his church home. When I look at the website of the church and I have visited the church, my heart is filled with joy and I am very proud to see how greatly God has blessed the church. I paid him the compliment of acknowledging how proud I was to see what has happened with the church. What he said to me in response to my words captured my heart and made me feel embraced and revitalized. He told me that a lot of what the church has become today was in many ways a result of what I helped it become the years I was there. Now while that may not mean much to most reading this, it meant the world to me. I felt so unworthy and removed because of everything I did before and because of the impact that it caused others. His words were just what I needed to feel connected again. After all, isn't that what we all look for, to be validated? Don't we all want to feel connected to God and to his work? You may have felt or are feeling a sense of disconnect. Perchance you may be the voice someone needs to hear to find their way back to God. Please understand God has always used people and will continue to use people to be the channel of His grace. To help people get to the restoration place in God.

CHAPTER SIX

THE RESTORATION PROJECT

"Have mercy upon me, O God, According to Your loving kindness; According to the multitude of Your tender mercies, Blot out my transgressions. Wash me thoroughly from my iniquity, and cleanse me from my sin. For I acknowledge my transgressions; and my sin is always before me. Against You and You only, have I sinned and done this evil in Your sight. That You may be found just when You speak and blameless when You judge. Behold, I was brought forth in iniquity and in sin did my mother conceive me. Behold, You desire truth in the inward parts, and in the hidden part You will make me to know wisdom. Purge me with hyssop, and I shall be clean: Wash me and I

shall be whiter than snow. Make me hear joy and gladness that the bones You have broken may rejoice. Hide Your face from my sins, and blot out all my iniquities. Create in me a clean heart, O God and renew a steadfast spirit within me. Do not cast me away from Your presence, and do not take away Your Holy Spirit from me. Restore to me the joy of Your salvation, and uphold me by Your generous Spirit. Then I will teach transgressors Your ways, and sinners shall be converted to You. Deliver me from the guilt of bloodshed, O God, The God of my salvation and my tongue shall sing aloud of Your righteousness. O Lord, open my lips, and my mouth shall show forth Your praise. For You do not desire sacrifice, or else I would give it; You do not delight in burnt offering. The sacrifices of God are a broken spirit, a broken and contrite heart. These, O God, You will not despise" (Psalms 51:1-17 NKJV).

THAT WAS MY FAULT

This scripture summarizes and underscores the thoughts and sentiments of David as it relates to how he addressed the shortcomings and sins of his life and his resolve to gain back the ground he lost. To really get an appreciation for where I am going with this scripture it may be a good idea to read about the situation that David created (2 Samuel 11 & 12). We must have acknowledgement, it is very critical in order for any level of restoration to be realized. There must first be recognition of the offense and the state of our existence. Whenever damage has occurred due to an offense within a relationship there can be no resolve or advancement until there is first an acknowledgement of the issue. No real healing can take place before someone addresses the hurt that was caused. Sometimes that can often pose the greatest challenge because it means coming to terms with something that reflects our imperfection. It may mean flying overhead and assessing and surveying the damage that our actions caused and then having to embrace the impact that it caused others. For those who tend to function as a perfectionist that is very difficult. For those who operate with a lot of pride it can be even more challenging. Often it is hard to embrace the acknowledgement because we may feel that it would make us look weak, incomplete, or incompetent. The reality is that when we truly measure ourselves next to God we are all weak, incomplete and incompetent. We need Him no matter what and we certainly come up short.

"For all have sinned and fall short of the glory of God" **(Romans 3:23 NKJV).**

"But we are all as an unclean thing, and all our righteousness are as filthy rags; and we all do fade as a leaf; and our iniquities, like the wind, have taken us away"(Isaiah 64:6 NKJV).

Typically when someone has felt the brunt of hurt or some type of offense there is a need for validation of the occurrence which has taken place. To refuse validation of someone else's hurt that you may have caused can simply be translated as an insult to their intelligence. This keeps us further separated from the person we have hurt. This includes our relationship with God. As hard as it may be to imagine, it is very possible to hurt God by our actions. I think the hardest thing for me was to look upon the impairment that choices in my life caused. The interesting thing about choices we make is that very seldom can we view the true outcome when we are making the initial decision. We perceive that the outcome will be favorable for ourselves or those involved. Most people in their right mind would never knowingly do something they knew would cause any severe devastation in someone else's life. But the hard reality is that it does happen whether it was intentional or not. You may never have intended to end up in the condition you may have found yourself in or currently find yourself in, but you have to be honest about where you stand no matter how hard it is to look at it. Sometimes doing what is right is the most difficult task of all. You can't clean up a mess you made on the carpet until you first acknowledge the spill.

When you look at the scripture noted above it summarizes the heart of one King David, who has been made to look at the results of a single decision that had catastrophic consequences. In David's pursuit a woman (Bathsheba) of his desires, he was so determined to get what he knew he could not lawfully have. While being drunk with his own power and position. David has her husband (Uriah) sent out to battle where he knew he would not survive. Consequently, Uriah is killed in battle and David moves in to take on his widow as his own. This of course was the decision he made once he discovered that she was pregnant with his child, after committing adultery.

THE PLAN

The issue here is David's motive. He experienced so much success from childhood to his adult life that he became consumed by his victories and accolades. He felt that there was nothing he could not have and if it wasn't his, he could make it his. Don't get me wrong, David loved God and was truly devoted to the things of God. He is one of the greatest kings to every address the throne in Israel. However, David was not perfect. He was a man flawed and in need of accountability. As I examined many of my own setbacks and the things that I ultimately lost, much of it was due to some sense of entitlement I felt I had. Typically what I was feeling was that whatever I planned to do I could do without any true sense of accountability or failure. Nobody plans to do anything they feel will fail or not succeed. My thoughts were that I could contain everything I was doing and keep it all under control. The truth of course is that I was not controlling my issues, but rather they were controlling me. I think that what we must be truly honest with is just who is controlling who. I believe we must monitor our sense to entitlement in life. Entitlement can become the gateway to pride if not kept in check.

David's plan was to conceal what he had done and he felt that somehow his secret would be buried with Uriah. Most people have skeletons in their closet and if others were to really discover them, they could cause the greatest embarrassment. I know that there are things that I have done in my life that I am not proud of and when I experienced those things I was just like David. Just bury it. Usually when something happens that we don't want people to find out about we do our best to bury the secret. The truth about secrets is that they always come out in the most inopportune moment. It is never convenient, but it will cause you the most embarrassment and put you in the most awkward position you can imagine. This is why it is always best to be honest about things you may have done. The truth is that everyone makes mistakes and people if they are honest about it will acknowledge that reality. I believe you have to learn to be honest within yourself before you can truly be honest with others. Self-honesty is sometimes more challenging because it requires resolve which can be so difficult at times to accomplish. Honesty of where you are in your current condition as it relates to a relationship or even a view of something that you feel or believe. It's not always easy, but it is necessary in the interest of personal advancement. I believe if we all were made to embrace the ultimate expression of truth that lies within us we would often find ourselves very challenged with enfolding what we find or what has been revealed. Quite frankly there are things within each of us that we find repulsive or unattractive. When it comes to our approach to God, He will not allow us to make pretense of our condition or mindset. He desires honesty no matter how difficult that may be to display. That means not only observing the great potential that lies within you but also examining the ugly places of your personality that require change and adjustment. It doesn't matter how perfect someone may appear on the outside, everyone has that place within them.

David puts it best in the text above, *"Behold, you desire truth in the inward parts"*. What I have learned is that most people will ultimately respect you more for your honesty rather than reject you for it. Unfortunately you can't share your secrets with everybody because not everyone has your best interest at heart nor is it wise to do so. But God can and does put people in your life that can often be a source of support to you as you share your experiences. Sometimes we can look passed people right next to us who would give us the audience to share our story and keep us protected from the onslaught of public opinion. Don't be so quick to run to someone that is in an esteemed position who doesn't really know you or even have an interest in you to share your secrets. Be willing to look at the person God may have blessed you with that could be right in front of you who won't judge you, but will pray and encourage you to do what is right. But make sure they have the spiritual maturity to guide and support you wisely and not further enable you down a negative or unproductive path.

From a Pastor's perspective, it was very difficult for me to find a Pastor that I could be that transparent with because there was the element of unspoken competition that often exists amongst Pastors. I also felt the fear of being rejected and scorned by some Pastors, which turned out to be a reality on one occasion. And, not to mention, the component of shame that accompanied my weaknesses. I felt like the situation would translate into Miranda law, what I said could and would be used against me in some form. That is very tragic because I often wonder just how many other Pastors have had to contend with the same type of problems I had, and have no one to share their burdens. You can research and utilize resources to try to gain an accurate assessment of the actual numbers of Pastors who find themselves in trouble with unmentionable circumstances, but chances are, the results would not be very accurate. Most Pastors would not dare divulge such transparent information. Pastors often lead very sheltered lives because of their positions. In fact I am sure many high level leaders across the management board share that same type of challenge. Pastors encourage their members to share in their burdens, but who is there for them to help them with their own burdens. Sometimes Pastors must reach across the country or the world to find that one person they can be transparent with, without fear of rejection and exploitation. In the end, we are all human and need to be able to share our experiences both good and bad with some- one who has our best interests at heart. Who is that person in your life?

Sometimes it does serve to help someone else as you reveal your more humanistic side. But if you are looking to share your "secrets" with someone please make sure that you are prayerful about, to whom you share your secrets. Be sure you do not share with someone that will ultimately use what you say against you. I have had that happen in the past and it was anything but pleasant. Make sure they are spiritually mature enough to pray with you through your issues and naturally mature enough to respect confidentiality.

When you plan to do things that you know are not godly or right towards other people, disaster is imminent and certain. It may not happen that moment or that day or month or even that year. But rest assured it is coming. The plans that we make depict our motives and sometimes our motives are not pure. I think I was often in denial of my motives and the reality and truth of what they were was not discovered until the calamity hit. Many people at your job, in your community, your family, or your church do not always possess the best motives. Whether it is the corporate Vice President, the politician, even the Pastor or the usher, everyone must check their motives. Whenever we begin attempting a new venture there is always an anticipation of what we hope to gain from our experience. The plans we make in life have a lot to do with and are reflective of our expectations. No one makes a plan without attaching an expectation to it. It doesn't matter if the expectations of those plans are for success or failure. An expectation is always associated with it. But just because we set our plans doesn't mean that they will align with God's plans. There were so many occasions when I thought or expected something to take place within a church service, and it would often end up going a different direction.

"A man's heart plans his ways but the Lord directs his steps" (Proverbs 16:9NKJV).

Ultimately we want God to be in full control over every step we make in life. He truly has your best interests at heart. Make sure the plans you make are God given and not merely self-gratifying. Don't make the mistake of making great plans and then asking God to bless them. Find out what His plan is for your life and seek to walk in it and you will find that it will be blessed.

FINDING CONTENTMENT

The real issue behind this situation is that what David possessed was not enough to keep him satisfied. David had several wives and yet what he yearned for was to have more. Contentment is something that many seek, but few ever really find. When contentment is gained in your life there really is a sense of fulfillment and peace that you can enjoy. What I found that I lacked for so many years was contentment. I wasn't content in so many areas and it caused me to ultimately lose more than I gained. If there is no contentment within, it is very hard to find it outwardly.

***"Godliness plus contentment is great gain"* (I Timothy 6:6 NKJV).**

Since so many things in our world are defined by what we possess it stands to reason that finding true contentment is a rare commodity. You get a small home and within a short time you want a bigger home. You may find yourself overcome with excitement because you finally got "a car" until you get used to it and then see someone with a nicer car. Suddenly your desire now shifts to get what you see someone else with. You fall in love and become devoted to your mate or spouse until you see someone else that seems to have what your mate or spouse doesn't. You can find that your desire for them diminishes as your curiosity of the other person increases. Stedman Graham once put it best, "what you focus on will expand". I believe most people feel that we are making good choices each day and that the path we are traveling is one that will lead us to a place of success and contentment. However, a lack of contentment can often drive us to poor choices. I am not suggesting that we settle for something less than what God may intend on us achieving in life. There is a difference between contentment and complacency.

What I am saying is that when our thoughts towards something that God has blessed us with become filled with disdain and/or discontentment we have lost our perspective on how great our gift really has been. And if we aren't careful we can exchange a blessing for a curse. One thing God will not do is make you keep what He has given you. You can keep it or exchange it or even lose it. I have certainly lost what was great in my life on several occasions simply because I lost perspective of how truly wonderful my blessing was. What is it in your life that may not appear as wonderful as it once was? Has that person or thing lost its value in your eyes or has your perspective changed? Contentment should be a valued component in your prayer request. Do not lose sight of the little things. They are often filled with the greatest treasure in life.

My father has a close friend that I know. I had an interesting conversation with him on one occasion. We all went out to dinner after attending a worship service and I sat next to him as we enjoyed a great meal. I admired him because of what I knew he had accomplished in life. He found great success and wealth in his career and business endeavors. He was able to acquire a beautiful second home in an exclusive area of Florida. He was able to pay more for his second home than many could get for their only home. But what I admired about him was that even though he had been blessed so wonderfully, he remained humble in his demeanor. In the conversation we had, I asked him about his home and complimented him on how beautiful it was. His response to me is what really captured my attention and has stuck with me ever since. He told me that he appreciated a time in his family's life when they had a house that was so small many of them had to sleep on the floor. He said they didn't have much but they were all much happier. I was stunned and amazed hearing that. I would have never guessed that was his resolve just by looking at what he had. If you saw the home you probably would agree with me. But it just goes to show you that you can't judge the book by its cover. With greater blessings come greater challenges. Be careful of what you pray for and never lose perspective of how great things can happen in small places. God has never found dissatisfaction in the small things, we have.

When I served as an Assistant Pastor the smaller church building we occupied in the beginning years of the ministry held some of the most intense and life changing experiences imaginable. We experienced the move of God in ways that still rivet my thoughts today. We saw many healings and elevated expressions of worship that would make one feel they were standing in the presence of God Himself. When we moved to a larger facility with more people in attendance certain things seemed to diminish and the services weren't quite the same. They weren't bad but they didn't seem to hold the same types of experiences. Something changed with the modification of our venue.

You may have a business you are trying to start and don't have much to work with. It really doesn't matter about the quantity of what you possess it's the quality that matters most. Everything that has become large was once started small. Don't despise small beginnings.

Find contentment no matter where you are in life because it will serve you well. You may be in a job that you once enjoyed, but now find yourself challenged just getting up in the morning to report to work. Remember how much of a blessing it was when you first got the job and hold on to that perspective. When God is ready He will bless you to move you into something that will be both a blessing for you and for others that you impact. Just your presence alone may be speaking to someone's life and encouraging them. We never know how what we do affects someone else.

"Not that I speak in regard to need, for I have learned in whatever state I am, to be content" **(Philippians 4:11 NKJV).**

If you lose your sense of contentment it can tempt you to walk away from something that was meant to bless your life and end up causing you greater heartache and regret.

HEADING THE WRONG WAY

I generally have a good sense of direction when I am driving on the highway, but unfortunately, my sense of direction on the road of life has not always been as strong. One day while I was driving in San Francisco visiting a friend of mine, I made a turn down a street that I recognized. As I started down the street I noticed that a lot of the people on the street were looking at me quite intensely. As I continued down the street some of the people began to shout out and wave at me as to get my attention, but I had no idea what they wanted. Since I didn't know them of course I wasn't going to stop to figure it out. I was the only car at the moment on the street but I couldn't figure out what all the commotion was all about until I looked up and suddenly there were 4 rows of cars heading directly at me. I was traveling down a one way street going the wrong way. I had to abruptly pull my car over to the curb before I wound up in a head on collision. It was amazing there was no indication that I was heading the wrong way with the exception of a few people that I could not hear screaming at me. I thought I was going the right way when I set my plans to move forward, but I ended up going the wrong way on a one way street. When I looked back at the situation I realized that there were signs stating that I was on a one way street. The problem was that I was not paying attention to the signs nor the people.

"There is a way that seems right to a man but its end is the way of death" **(Proverbs 14:12 NKJV).**

Sometimes the reason we end up in the worst of circumstances is because we refused to read the signs or listen to the voices God placed in our lives that would offer us the greatest protection. I believe you can become so preoccupied with your personal agenda that you can miss out on vital information that would be of great benefit to you and to other people in your life. What is it that you may not pay attention to that could be the key to your greatest blessing? What are the signs you have prayed for but have paid little or no attention to? What you don't know could devastate your life. Your greatest opportunities could simply pass you by if you don't watch for even the simplest things that God may be placing in your life to help you advance in life. My biggest wrecks in life were never in my vehicle, but in my decisions. Those wrecks left me and others severely injured and damaged. Sadly in some cases, even death in relationships. It would require years of therapy to heal from the incidents. How many people have been adversely impacted by your choices? If we learn nothing else it is imperative that we learn to read the signs in life that are in place to protect us. It is never easy to resolve personal responsibility, but yet it is necessary to get to the next steps in life. God will not move to truly bless us until we first address our condition.

When David begins to write Psalm 51, the first thing he is pleading for is God's mercy. Mercy is what keeps us from getting what we deserve. David recognized the fact he was guilty. He took a wrong turn down a one way street in life. What was the sign that he ignored? Exodus 20:14 *"You shall not commit adultery"*. He does not try to make any excuses he simply takes full responsibility for his actions. Mercy is what you seek when you realize you have nothing else to aide you in your cause and you are completely and fully exposed to the reality of failure. A plead for mercy is given when you have no further defense to offer concerning what you have done. When you are confronted by God concerning wrong in your life and you are dealing with Him face to face, there are no resources or excuses that you can draw from that will assist you in your attempt to cover yourself. The best and only thing you can really do is to come clean with God. Our negative choices impact other people, but ultimately they are the greatest offenses toward God. For several years I attempted to get my life down the path of what I considered being normal. I wanted so much to see my church and life blessed. The problem was not in what I wanted to do. The issue was that there were so many unresolved areas that God still wanted me to address first. When we neglect areas that have incubated in our personal lives for years without giving them proper attention for a healthy resolve, we set ourselves and relationships up for problems and failures. Unhealthy cycles will only continue until there is a full healthy resolve in addressing issues that often stem back to our childhood.

THE FIRST STEPS

As I pointed out, acknowledgement is the first key to reconciliation. If we truly want to see restoration in our lives we must be willing to go to the extents necessary to promote healing and re-establishment. They are often challenging steps but important steps. Nothing would be blessed in my life until I first did my part in attempting to bring resolve in areas that negatively affected other people's lives. One such area concerned my children. When they were born I was right there to watch them enter the world and I was one of the first to hold them. When they were very small I buried myself deeply into their lives and interacted with them in as many ways as I could because of my love for them. This drew me very close to them and we enjoyed a very strong relationship. I taught them to ride bikes and roller blade. At Christmas I got on the floor and played with them. When my son was old enough I taught him and coached him in little league basketball.

Because of the choices I made, it took me away from my children and I became very much the absent father that so many children deal with today. It was never my intention to be absent from them, but no matter what, I loved them. After years of not being there as they grew older I lost what could never be replaced. The valuable time every child deserves and needs from their parent and some never find. When my daughter was thirteen I lived in Florida trying to live my life in a way that would somehow smooth over the mistakes that I made, before moving there, from California.

Through a horrific and emotionally devastating experience she was molested by a man that once attended the church I pastored. He was a much older man and knew better. While I realize there are things that perhaps I could not control or prevent, I couldn't help but feel completely overwhelmed by guilt for not being there to protect my baby girl from something so demoralizing and damaging. Though the circumstances were very earth shattering for her and my son, as well as their mother and I, it was nothing but the grace of God that got her through the situation. Today my daughter is living a life very committed to God and is very passionate about her relationship with Him. But during that time, my absence was quickly translated into abandonment, from their per-spective, and I felt the brunt of their anger and resentment. Don't get me wrong they were and are very respectful children (well actually young adults now), but their passive aggressive ways made it evident that they were deeply hurt and not pleased with me nor my decisions, which impacted them. There were fewer calls from them and often strained conversations that were never deeper than general com-munications. As time passed, I felt so sorrowful that I was not there to watch them experience the teenage years that are so critical for their nurturing.

In the interest of repairing damaged rela-tionships I knew I would have to do something that would show my children and God that I really cared and loved them deeply. For me it was very important that I examine my motives and take the steps necessary to reach out to them. This could not be handled over the phone, I needed to see them. I humbled myself and sucked up my pride and decided to take a trip back to California where they lived, to see them. As I would do with others, I met with both of them alone and acknowledged every-thing I did that impacted them and humbly asked for forgiveness. I knew that it would not immediately take away the pain they both felt from my actions, but it was a step in the right direction. I wanted to show them both just how much I loved them and was committed to seeing healing in our relationships so I could enjoy some of the most special moments in their lives as they got older. Finally, as I watched them come visit me when I lived in Atlanta one by one they both shared with me their desire to be closer to me. Though they both never pressured me I wanted to show them just how much they both meant. So I assured them both that in time I would find a way to be closer to them. When an unfortunate turn of events took place with my job and home I turned my face towards California and made my way back home. Though it wasn't easy to make the decision, it was the right decision. Today we talk more than we ever have and healing has drawn us much closer than we have been since they were small children.

If you desire to see relationships restored that may have been damaged from your choices, the best decision you could make for yourself is reaching out. This may mean having to humble yourself to do so, but trust me it is always worth it in the end. In this world where everyone wants to be proven right, acknowledging error on your part is very under rated. It is the bridge that helps to take us to restoration. While it certainly takes both parties to make it all work, in the end, what you must honestly assess is whether or not you have done your part in doing all that you can to bring healing.

David found forgiveness with God after he acknowledged his sins, but he still had to confront life's consequences. God would not let him off the hook. He lost the child that Bathsheba gave birth to. There was also great contention in his house amongst his older children. The challenges of dealing with consequences were evident but through it all God was always with David and still referenced him as a man after his own heart.

Perhaps we feel we want to be free from responsibility after we have wronged God or others, but consequences are often the tool that really teaches us humility and wisdom. Sometimes we can confuse forgiveness with consequences. Just because we may have been forgiven by God for actions we have taken, there may still be more required. The extent of consequences we are made to face is based upon the actions we have taken. Here is the hard truth about negative actions. No one gets away with anything. It can often appear that someone may get away with something they have done wrong, but in truth they don't. God always has a way with bringing back our offenses to make us deal with it. The problem is when we know what someone has done to us or someone we know and we can't watch them pay or suffer for it. God is not going to always put it on display and so we can find some sense of satisfaction in their agony.

However, the thing that someone has done that may have hurt you will never be pushed under the rug in God's eyes. Everyone pays one way or another. What I went through in payment for my sins were not witnessed by everyone I hurt. But believe me I paid for it and in many ways I am still paying for it. God does not intend for everyone to see what others go through because in many cases He wants to teach us forgiveness, true forgiveness and self-reflection. David's consequences would carry over passed his generation and yet he is noted as one of the greatest kings of Israel. He was not defined by his mistakes but rather by his resolve to be found honorable in God's eyes despite his mistakes. We can certainly learn from that lesson.

RESTORING PROCESS

One thing we can learn from David's avowal is that after acknowledging an offense there should be a cry for cleansing. Nothing can be fully restored until there is first a stripping of the weathered paint chips of our life's scars. Your life may feel weather beaten and distressed from all the many things you have gone through. Perhaps it is from a failed or abusive current marriage or relationships or on your job or even in church. The pervasive winds of life that have blown everything into complete disarray may have left you in a wounded, confused and bewildered state in life's existence. Perhaps it has left you angry and bitter towards people or even God. Maybe the thought of engaging in a relationship with someone or trusting people sends a river of pain right through your very being. There is a need for restoration. David's call for cleansing was recognition that if he were to be effective as a king and servant of God and His people he would first need to be cleansed. This would not make him less of a man, but it would make him more respected as a king. God knows much better how to clean us up than we do. Our efforts are always futile when it relates to doing it our way versus His way.

The breaking of bones that David refers to in Psalm 51 as being initiated by God is a recognition of the pride and arrogance stemming from his efforts in life, that David once stood upon as a foundation. We can often function under the same type of disposition that turns the face of God away from our lives.

"God resist the proud but gives grace to the humble" (James 4:6 NKJV).

God can't and will not work with pride and arrogance. His heart is moved whenever we are willing to humble ourselves. Someone once said that if you don't humble yourself in life, then life will humble you. Humility should not be considered weakness rather it is an acknowledgement of strength beyond your own. Pride and arrogance always suggests self-ability, self-reliance, and self-existence beyond God. While it is good to recognize your skill set and gifting, never make the mistake to think that it should be exercised absent of God's input and desire for your life.

"Trust in the Lord with all your heart and lean not to your own understanding but in all your ways acknowledge Him and He shall direct your path" (Proverbs 3:5-6 NKJV).

Don't allow yourself to become so consumed by your successes in life that you forget to stay connected to the one who blessed you with such grand opportunities. I am not speaking of just simple church attendance as a form of recognition, but rather a heartfelt personal fellowship that cannot be measured by the greatest worship services.

Once David's call for the pride and arrogance in his life to be broken, he then pleaded to God for his heart to be cleansed and his spirit to be made honorable. I cannot emphasize the necessity for this cry enough. God always looks at a person's heart beyond anything else. You will not be able to stand before God and flex your worldly accomplishments in front of Him as a form of validation. If your heart is not right with him your successes mean nothing. Hiding behind your corporate positioning or community position or church position will not give you the type of true cleansing that is needed to keep you right in His eyes. Believe me, you can hold a position in all areas of society and be completely out of position with God. Many people make the mistake of trying to find justification in faithful worship service attendance. That will not do it. Believe me I have tried it. If you find yourself in an uplifting service on Sunday and completely depressed by Monday something is out of alignment.

When I was in a car accident right before moving from Atlanta I didn't realize how much damage was done to my body at the moment of impact. Someone insisted that I go to the hospital because they felt it would be in my best interest. I thought I was strong enough to handle it without that experience. However, when I got there and they took x-rays it was discovered that I had minor whiplash. If you have ever been in a car accident you know that the pain is always worse the day after the accident than it is when it happens. There was more damage to my back than I knew. Today I still deal with some discomforts because of the accident. Consequently, I had to see a chiropractor to align my body so there would be normal fluidity of my body and less pain.

Sometimes we can find ourselves out of alignment with God and life without realizing how severe the damage may be that we have sustained. There are implications to every action we take in life. Some are good and some are not so good. Sometimes when we experience very negative things in our life the damage created from those situations can often appear down the road. Many times it is reflective in our relationships with others and may not have been previously obvious to us until certain circumstances bring them out.

The challenge with the restoration process is the addressing of painful places. Reminders of things we would rather forget. It has been the most uncomfortable place for me personally, but I have found that it has been the most rewarding and necessary place I had to go to help me move on. It served as a barometer of just how well I got over the negative things that impacted my life. Since we have all done things that we are not proud of or even feel ashamed of, it is important that we overcome the negative stigma that often accompanies the thoughts of those experiences. That is not always easy and sometimes they pose the greatest challenges. But in order to advance further into areas that would be a blessing in our lives and the lives of others it sometimes means allowing God to deal with us in areas we don't want to go. If you find yourself in that place as you read this, pray and ask God to help you look upon the necessary places and to help you address the things needed to bring healing and restoration of joy to those areas of your life.

RESTORING THE JOY

Where David found solace was asking God to restore back to him the joy of God's salvation. I thought upon that scripture for many years and could never fully comprehend what it meant. That was until I found myself wrestling to enter into a worship service again. For so many years I came to church faithfully and served in the ministry and did anything that was asked of me and even beyond the call of duty. But yet there was still great emptiness inside of me. The emptiness started out small and expanded over time. Setback after set-back, challenge after challenge. With each unfortunate experience my joy seemed to become consumed by an ever increasing sense of emptiness. Even quoting scriptures did not seem to make the impact I longed for and needed become a reality in my life. Have you ever found yourself in that place? Are you currently in that place? At some point I asked myself as I reasoned with not going to church, "isn't there more to this than what I am experiencing?" What was once a sincere place of worship became the place where I could put on my mask. The closer I got towards the end of attending church services, the more clever the disguises became.

Church services eventually became an experience of nothing but clichés and religiously pious showmanship. I became skeptical of much of what I saw. I saw many religious programs on television as marketing opportunities for various ministries. While you could make an argument of that notion, my condition just heightened my resolve. It was so easy to become critical and cynical of everything that took place in a worship service. It would get to the point where I would sum up everything before the worship team could even begin the first song. I continued to insist that the church was missing something. In truth it wasn't that the church was missing something. It was that I was missing something. Something I had not experienced in many years.

The empty place that David felt was based on the reality that he missed God in a great capacity. Sometimes it takes embracing something that reflects hard truth. David would face severe consequences for his actions even though God would forgive him for the sins. But before any consequences would be experienced God told him what the offense was. When God looks to scrape away the debris from our life He ensures that we are made aware of what that debris is. If we are honest with ourselves we usually know what it is before He has to address it. The problem, typically exists when we refuse to deal with something that God eventually has to address. When you read about the encounter David had with Nathan (a prophet of God) who brought this matter to his attention, David is very critical and judgmental of the person Nathan used as an example to bring his point home. Nathan used a fictional story or a parable to illuminate the situation to David. David felt it easier to hide behind the fault of a fictitious person rather than deal with his own mistake. As long as he thought it was someone else at fault of an injustice he was ready to pronounce harsh sentencing and execution on the person. When it was brought to his attention that he was the focal point of the story and it was really all about him and what he did the walls of reality and truth came crashing upon him. He now feels completely incredulous with guilt and sorrow.

In grappling with where we fall short with God, it can feel overwhelming just embracing what has been lacking or wrong in our life. It isn't easy to face the fact that you may have drifted away from God. In truth everyone can stand to get closer to God. The issue is when you suddenly have found yourself much further than you ever thought you would be.

What I feel we must measure is, how much of the joy we may have once experienced in our relationship with God has been lost, due to the challenges of life. It isn't always so obvious when we lose something that is so precious and valuable. It wasn't until I sat back and looked hard at what slipped away from me that I realized how it left me in the first place. The truth was not that someone took it from me. I wasn't robbed by the people's objections to my role in church. It wasn't because of jealousy or apparent successes in ministry that I lost the joy. It was because I stopped doing what allowed me to experience the joy in the first place.

There was a time when I would spend precious time alone with God in such a way that I felt complete and fulfilled. When I would attend services in those days I would often make sure that my wife and children were fed after service and settled in for the rest of the day. I would get in my car on occasion and drive away to secluded locations and meditate on what I experienced that day. I would often thank God for everything He blessed me with and wittingly try to get closer to Him through my prayers and meditation. Each time I did that, whether in my car or in one of the bedrooms alone, I always stood back up feeling a sense of peace I cannot possibly put into words. It left me feeling so complete and fulfilled regardless of what may have not been going so well in my life. I found the treasure of God's joy in those silent moments of solitude.

It was so simple, but I somehow allowed it to drift away from me unintentionally. I got lazy and distracted by the issues of the daily routines. No one took it away from me, I gave it up. I pressed on faithfully serving God in weekly church services, but never spending the time with Him that He enjoyed even more than I did. I often wonder how many Pastors and leaders in church get so caught up into what they do weekly that they just may be experiencing many of the same things I felt.

When you stop and think about it, what strengthens any relationship? Time and communication, when you take those things away the relationship suffers and you can find that you aren't enjoying the closeness that you once did. Did you know that God can hurt just like you can? Think about someone you love more than words can express and how you would feel if they suddenly stopped talking to you and didn't want to spend time with you. What if you gave them things and they refused to thank you or acknowledge that you did anything for them. How would it make you feel? Certainly this thought is subjective, but I'm sure you can understand my point. God values our time with Him and when that is suddenly lost due to things and people we allow to rob us, that joy gets lost in the process. His joy and ultimately ours is lost as well. Things are never the same when His joy leaves us. This is why David's plea to God was "Do not cast me from your presence and do not take your Holy Spirit away from me". It is so easy to take for granted all of the many wonderful things God has done for us in our lives. But when ingratitude settles in and distractions change our perspective on the most delicate of things in our lives. We can find ourselves feeling completely hopeless and vulnerable. It has often been said that the Holy Spirit is a gentleman and will not force Himself on anyone. He is gentle but the bottom line is that God will not force you nor me to do anything. We either willingly invite Him into our world or He will stand back and watch us from a distance.

David's biggest fear was not the loss of wealth or his kingdom. His biggest fear was his loss of relationship with God. The thought of that carries a hurt that is very difficult to describe. Perhaps you may have experienced that or reading this now, are feeling that way. The security we enjoy from a healthy relationship with God is paramount to our peace and daily existence. If you have found yourself in that place of lacking the joy of God's salvation you can get it restored. You must be willing to go to the place that you once valued and make the time to spend getting closer than you ever have before.

Today I have found that turning off the television and phones and ipods to give God that valuable time has proven to be a priceless decision. Every week I take long walks on the beach alone at a location I frequented growing up. I make my way out to a jetty and sit on the rocks and watch the sun begin its decent on the day. As I sit there, I thank God for everything I can conceivably think of. My prayers are mostly filled with gratitude rather than requests. Requests that are made are for other people and also things that will make me a better person and not just for something material. I pray for things like wisdom and understanding because those things will get me through life and not just another car. I have found that God's joy has nothing to do with the next house we get or career opportunity or achieving some elevated social status. It has to do with being in a certain place, with Him that is much more fulfilling than anything we can get our hands on. Everything has its place but nothing can replace the feeling you get when you have discovered the joy of God's salvation. The joy of the Lord is your strength.

THE QUALIFIED TEACHER

As David examined the benefit of experiencing the rekindling of God's presence in his life he knew that a new lesson would be realized. Something that he was not previously qualified for was now within his reach. His awakening regarding his actions certainly took him from a confident leader to a humbled servant. There was recognition that sometimes our actions can remove us from certain opportunities we might otherwise enjoy. I think sometimes we can become so obsessed with achieving successes in life that we can miss valuable lessons along the way. It wasn't that David wasn't a great leader, the bigger issue was that his gifting and positioning were not tempered by humility as they once were. It was David's humility and passion for God that captured His heart and attention in the beginning. It would take that again to regain the benefits of servitude. This time David would be able to share a perspective about God that would now turn the hearts of men towards heaven.

When you look at this situation from God's perspective David was shut down completely from hearing the things that God would say to him. Things that could have prevented the mistake that would plague David's reign for years to come. But when you are in a place where you have known nothing but success, and things that may have been difficult for most to acquire, come very easily to you, it is possible that you can become so self-reliant that the need for calling on God seems to fade. In essence the temptation of success is to lose a hunger for God. The question is, can you walk in pride without realizing how much it has a grip on you? I believe it is possible.

As I thought about where I was several years ago, it became evident that I was a teacher who needed to be taught. I often felt the need to be right because I never wanted to be proven wrong. I enjoy listening to people because I feel that you can learn so much more by listening rather than talking. But I find it amazing that when it came to the doing what would have helped me to improve my quality of life, I really struggled to listen when it was most important. I guess you can say that in a way I was sabotaging my own blessings in life. Perhaps much of it came from feeling that I was unworthy or didn't deserve such good things in my life. I felt that so many people had ill motives and really were attempting to say things to control my actions. The problem that I had with it was that I refused to be controlled; therefore, I would not hear what was being said to me. Now I do believe God puts people in our lives that serve as instruments to guide us down the best paths possible for our purpose. But when you are resolved not to embrace what those voices may have to say, you can cut off your own blessings. The problem with this was that it prevented me from maximizing what could not only be beneficial for me, but also limiting what I had to offer to others.

I think if we are not careful we can shut off something that God intends to use to bless others simply by refusing to hear what someone has to say. Have you ever found yourself in that position? Perhaps it's time to start listening.

David implied that if God were to restore his life it would give him a testimony unmatched by his previous victories. Remember, David was best known for gaining the attention of God to become one of the youngest rulers to sit on the throne of Israel. Not to mention his famous slaying of Goliath at age 17. He became so victorious in battle as he grew older, that the citizens of Israel created a song celebrating the fact that his kills greatly outnumbered those of King Saul which infuriated the then king. He was famously known for his expressive acts of worship and praise before God. There was no question in anyone's mind that David loved God. But none of his accomplishments and successes through the battlefield of life could compare to the thought of his sentiment, which was to teach transgressors the ways of God and see sinners' hearts turned towards God. Ultimately, what was most important to David was to see the lives of people changed by them drawing closer to God. It certainly puts everything into perspective. What David would be able to share with people was far different after his fall, than before.

Experiencing triumphant goals you may have planned for yourself is one thing, but getting closer to God is another. When I went through some of my lowest points and sat in counseling one of the things that encouraged me so much was hearing something people would say to me on different occasions. "One day people will be blessed by your story and I can't wait to see what God does." I have never forgotten that and it carried me through so many of my low points. What it said is that God was not finished with me. What I can clearly say today is that through God's loving mercy and grace my voice is stronger today than it has ever been. Let me encourage you as you read this and let you know that just because you may have made some bad choices in your life, your story isn't over, it's just beginning.

Education gives you the tools to succeed in life, but challenges give you the passion to change lives. Your circle of influence may be small or large but what qualifies you to positively alter someone's life for the better is being restored to a place in God where He can use you in ways you never thought possible. **Don't hide from your past, make it work for you**.

What David's conclusion finally showed was that while God appreciates faithful service in our lives and a strong diligence to even come to His house for worship service, it is the posturing of our heart that grabs His attention. Whenever we make a mistake or offend God in any way we must put everything we do in proper alignment and perspective so that God can receive what we give Him. When I finally hit rock bottom in ministry, I kept trying to offer up what I thought was acceptable worship. It was anything but acceptable. What I feel we often strive for is perfection. We want perfection in our careers, our relationships, our images, even in our church attendance and participation. But in truth God never expected perfection from us. If we were perfect would there be a need for Jesus Christ to have come and died for us?

"For the law made nothing perfect; on the other hand there is the bringing in of a better hope, through which we draw near to God" **(Hebrews 7:19NKJV).**

The call for our perfection in the Bible is better translated as maturity. Many people have made the mistake of feeling that if they can get themselves together first, then they can come to God. You will never be able to get yourself cleaned up on your own. It takes much more than what you and I have to offer God. There is only one thing you can give God when you find yourself in the worst condition. As your true gift, offer God your heart, humbled and broken, not some futile attempt to cover up the stench of life that may cover you. Be honest with yourself and be honest with God and it will make you honest with others.

"Then He said: "A certain man had two sons. And the younger of them said to his father, Father give me the portion of goods that falls to me." So he divided to them his livelihood. And not many days after the younger son gathered all together, journeyed to a far country, and there wasted his possessions with prodigal living. But when he had spent all, there arose a severe famine in that land, and he began to be in want. Then he went and joined himself to a citizen of that country, and he sent him into his fields to feed swine. And he would gladly have filled his stomach with the pods that the swine ate, and no one gave him anything. But when he came to himself, he said, How many of my father's hired servants have bread enough and to spare and I perish with hunger! I will arise and go to my father and will say to him, "Father, I have sinned against heaven and before you, and I am no longer worthy to be called your son. Make me like one of your hired servants." And he arose and came to his father. But when he was still a great way off, his father saw him and had compassion, and ran and fell on his neck and kissed him. And the son said to him, "Father, I have sinned against heaven and in your sight, and am no longer worthy to be called your son." But the father said to his servants, "Bring out the best robe and put it on him, and put a ring on his hand and sandals on his feet and bring the fatted calf here and

kill it, and let us eat and be merry; for this my son was dead and is alive again; he was lost and is found." And they began to be merry" (Luke 15:11-24NKJV).

The truth behind this parable taught by Jesus is God's mindset as it relates to restoration. I felt like I lived it out in so many ways. Perhaps you may have found yourself in the same position.

The parable is the story of a wealthy man who had two sons. The younger of the two wanted his inheritance early and insisted that his father give him what he felt was rightfully his. Once he received it he left his father and began living life in the most irresponsible manor and doing things contrary to what he knew to be right. It was all about him and he was merely living a very selfish lifestyle. Eventually he winds up broke living in a foreign place dealing with people who don't love him as his father did. He takes on a job tending to pigs. This was considered the lowest form of social existence. It is a drastic reduction from how he was raised or what was expected of him. We are not told how long he was gone and living in that condition. The idea is that we all can suffer the same fate and while time frames can change from person to person we are all just a step away from being in place of debased living. You may be reading this and find yourself in that place today. The good news my friend is that you can come out of it today.

When people are incarcerated particularly for extended periods of time, seldom does anyone leave "rehabilitated". This is because the prison system is not designed for nor is there true interest in rehabilitation. On the contrary it is expected that many will wind back up in the prison system. The issue is not the condition of the prison system or the condition of the society they may be returning to, the real issue is the condition of the heart. You see until we honestly come to grips with where our heart lies, nothing really will change in the outcomes of our lives. This is why you can change a person's venue, but you certainly can't change their heart. If you changed the person's heart the person can change the culture of their venue.

In the story Jesus told, the youngest son gets to the point that he realizes that he has settled for less than what his father intended for him and he compromised all that he knew was right. His selfish choices landed him in a lifestyle he would have never imagined he would be in. Have you ever found yourself in a situation like that? Have you ever questioned how you ended up doing or living in a way that was anything but what you dreamed of growing up? I certainly did. There were moments where I asked myself, "What am I doing here?" It was anything but ideal and very challenging to look at. All of these experiences were due to choices I selfishly made that I thought would give me what I wanted in life. Each time I made a decision I made it with the intent of proving that I was making the right move for my life. But each time I eventually lost out on what was beneficial in my life.

GIVE UP TO GET MORE

When all of the son's means were fully exhausted and he found himself eating from the same source of food as the pigs ate, he finally had an epiphany. Realizing that he was living in a way that was completely unacceptable and even more significant, unnecessary, he began to reflect on the one person that loved him above any other, his father. Recognizing that his father's employees had it better than him, he postured himself to return home. The move would require humility and courage, but when you have lost all that you have in life it becomes much easier to humble yourself. Upon his return his father saw him coming from a distance and had deep compassion for his son. The reason this is so important is because many people fear going to God and often others when they have drifted away or have never come to Him, out of a fear of rejection and humiliation. I lost out on many things in life over the past several years so, I got to the point where I was willing to do whatever I needed to do to find God's grace again in my life. It was the most precious thing I seemed to have lost. I was in such need of restoration. I needed something no other person could give me. A great job or home or relationship would not do it for me. I needed the relationship that I had with my heavenly father fully restored. I was tired of feeling like a disgraced Pastor and a failed father and a failed son, brother, husband and friend.

The only way I would possibly get to a place of peace and positive resolve was to leave the place that was foreign to me and return to the soothing arms of a very loving Father. I was willing to leave what I had to get more of what I needed. Many people do not intentionally seek to drift away or leave God. Our choices can do that without us really sentient to that fact. There are those who have drifted away or walked away from God because they were or are angry with or have just stopped believing in Him. Whatever your plight, just know that you can return to Him without fear of rejection or ridicule. When you read the remainder of the parable Jesus is speaking about the most encouraging part of the story which is the reaction of the father. Once he recognizes his son from a far distance he doesn't wait for his son to get close to him he comes out to meet his son and immediately falls on his neck kissing and hugging him out of pure relief and gratitude. It becomes unclear who is more grateful. The son or the father, the beauty of this story is that both desired reconciliation and restoration of the relationship.

Here is the truth of the matter. When two people really do love each other no matter what the disagreement there is typically a longing to see what was enjoyed between the two parties restored. God's desire for you and me is to see us close to Him no matter what. You may be reading this and feel so far away from God because of your life's choices and current condition. Just know that God wants to see you closer to Him than you have ever been or imagined. It really does not matter what you have done in your life, He still wants you and loves you beyond words. If you are still here and reading this, you are because of God's passion for you.

The real question concerning the restoration of our lives is, does God desire perfection from us? The answer is absolutely no. God certainly does not expect us to live a perfect life or to be perfect. It isn't an issue of perfection with God it's an issue of being found acceptable to God. One of the issues that has often clouded the minds of many is the clarification of what it means to live a life that is holy. For years I confused holiness with perfection. It has caused a great rift between many people of the Christian community whose interpretation of holiness has often varied. God only had one example of the perfect man and he has come and gone and will return one day, and that is Jesus Christ. Until then we are all works in progress. After all, restoration is a continual process faithfully being worked by the hand of God and will not be completed until we are standing before Him, face to face.

No matter what your role may be in this life or your affiliation, restoration is God's plan for your life. Be willing to spend quiet time in meditation and prayer and you will find that much of what you have lost in your connection will begin to return to your life. There is nothing wrong with seeking to gain success in life, but allow the success to be bathed in the confidence of a close fellowship with God. That is where you will find your true sense of contentment.

About the Author

As a native of California, Randy was born and raised in Los Angeles. At the age of 19, he received his calling to serve God as a minister of the gospel. In 1984, he began serving his country in the United States Air Force and was honorably discharged after six years receiving various awards for his service, including the Air Force Commendation medal. In 1992, at the Center of Praise Ministries in Sacramento, California he served as an Associate Pastor and eventually became the Assistant Pastor under the leadership of Bishop Parnell M. Lovelace, Jr. In 1994, Pastor Dean and Bishop Lovelace received their International License and Ordination with the International Church of the Foursquare Gospel. In 1997, Pastor Dean went on to pioneer and pastor Hope Center Ministries in Elk Grove, California. In 2002, after moving to Tampa, Florida he began pastoring Hope Center International Ministries. He currently serves as the Executive Assistant to Bishop Milton S. Herring, I, with Advancing the Kingdom of God Ministries (ATKOG) based in Torrance, California.

Pastor Dean has been noted as being a speaker that utilizes depth in and comprehensive understanding of the word of God to impart relevant messages that are underscored with humor to reach people of all cultures and age groups. His ability to conceptualize church development and spiritual growth dynamics has served to benefit everyone who has sat under his teachings.

He is the father of two children Steven and Ashli Dean of Sacramento, California. He currently resides in his hometown of Los Angeles, California.

PUBLISHER PAGE

All scripture references were taken from the New King James Version of the Bible.

Publishing – Create Space

Editing – D. Rene' Woods

He Restores My Soul is also available:

Audio through Ibooks and CD's

Kindle and Ebooks

For more information or bookings please visit our website:

www.randysteven.com

REAR COVER

If you have ever found yourself questioning the validity of your relationship with God or wondering if the mistakes you have made in the past somehow disqualified you from being viewed as His son or daughter, you certainly want to look at this perspective. Have you ever wondered how many Pastors and other Leaders in church ultimately found themselves at the forefront for public humiliation through moral failure? This book offers an insightful and realistic look at the dynamics of the walk of Christian believers and the Leadership within the local church. It is unusually transparent as Randy Dean shares experiences from a Pastors perspective that offers illumination to all who look to draw a closer walk in their relationship to God. Instead **He Restores My Soul** underscores and expresses God's desire to not only rekindle the relationship between Him and His creation but to restore the relationship to an unprecedented level and maximize the potential you were created for.

"This book is a timely resource for all who read it, especially those serving in ministry. Pastor Randy unmask the enemy we all deal with at some point in our lives, the perversion of our sexual capacities. In a very transparent way, he walks us through his valley of darkness, and leads us to the light of God's amazing grace. Read it with an open and non-judgemental heart. This book may be an answered prayer for you or someone you know".

Bishop Milton S. Herring, I

Advancing The Kingdom of God Ministries